Signs For Me

Basic Sign Vocabulary
for
Children, Parents & Teachers

Ben Bahan & Joe Dannis

DawnSignPress

Sign Language Clowns reprinted with permission, *Ralph R. Miller, Sr.*
Edited by *Tina Jo Breindel*
Cover Illustrations by *Brian Clarke, Frank Allen Paul*
Illustrations by *Brian Clarke, Betty Miller, Frank Allen Paul*
Sign Illustrations by *Rob Hills, Frank Allen Paul, Daniel W. Renner, Paul Setzer, Peggy Swartzel-Lott*

Sign Models:

Chernet Campbell   *Amanda Cervi*   *Anthony Kolombatovic*

Nikko Norman-Peterson   *Erin Paul*   *Karina Peterson*   *A.G. Woodford*

ISBN: 0-915035-27-8

Library of Congress Catalog Card Number: 0-081463

10 9 8 7 6 5

——— ATTENTION: SCHOOLS & DISTRIBUTORS: ———

Quantity discounts for schools and bookstores are available.
For information, please contact:

DawnSignPress

ORDER TOLL FREE! 1-800-549-5350

Monday-Friday: 8am to 4pm Pacific Time

*This book is dedicated
in memory of FAP
who gave us our start . . .*

Contents

Foreword   vii

Introduction   ix

Verbs   1

Adjectives   25
    Feelings   26
    Opposites   34

Nouns   49
    People   50
    Family   63
    Transportation   67
    House   71
    Safety   80
    Toys   83
    Animals   87
    Plants   98

Pronouns   101

Number Signs   106

American Manual Alphabet   107

Indexes   108
    ASL   108
    English   111
    Spanish   112
    Cambodian   113
    Hmong   114
    Lao   115
    Tagalog   116
    Vietnamese   117

Foreword

Signs for Me is the first in a planned series of books that presents American Sign Language in a clearly defined, accessible format. ASL is the language used by the majority of Deaf people in the United States. It takes advantage of visual and spatial properties of language as opposed to spoken languages which utilize auditory and vocal features. Although this language is used as the natural language of Deaf people, the previous decade has seen a tremendous explosion in the learning and use of ASL by hearing people. Colleges, universities and schools for the Deaf offer classes in ASL which has resulted in a rapid increase in the number of ASL users. Through television, the media, the National Theatre of the Deaf, and numerous other groups, public awareness about the Deaf Community and their language has increased significantly. Deaf children, at a much younger, age are beginning to have access to many of the varied avenues in which information is transferred. The dawning of the age of Deaf people has just begun.

It is with excitement and commitment that this book has been developed and presented in honor of young deaf children in the United States and the world. Development has proceeded over the previous five years with the intention of producing an intellectual and accessible system for learning ASL and concurrently learning how English is translated into ASL.

We believe we have achieved our goal in this first issue. The book was developed to provide access to the world around young Deaf children, to enhance their language abilities while they are very young, to encourage them to explore and yearn for more, and to provide a base in which parents and children can learn together.

Parents were a central concern in the development of the format of this book. *Signs for Me* is a guide; it is a beginning. It is our hope that the book will be used as a tool to increase interactions and result in stronger bonds between parents and their deaf children.

Signs for Me is also intended to provide a mechanism for teachers to identify and construct grammatical lessons in ASL similar to what is done for the teaching of English. This will be one of the first texts that educationally includes ASL in the same manner as English. The 1990's will be the decade of ASL in the education programming for Deaf children.

This is one of the first bilingual/bicultural books for the young deaf child to use at home and at school. I am confident that you will find this a useful tool and an excellent guide for young Deaf children to begin their experiences in ASL and at the same time begin to understand how English relates to this rich visual language.

Robert J. Hoffmeister, Ph.D.
Boston University

Introduction

This book began in a little house by the sea in San Diego, California. It was not developed by accident like some well-known invention stories in which a scientist inadvertently spilled a test tube of erroneously mixed formula on a counter and created a product that became a marketable giant in this consumer crazed world.

It was, however, by accident that three people came together to create this book—Frank Allen Paul, the artist whose vision set forth the beauty of this book, Ben Bahan whose expertise in language acquisition, bilingualism and American Sign Language who spurred the critical incorporation of ASL and English in this book for Deaf children in both home and school settings, and Joe Dannis, a publisher who has the means for pulling this book together and an eye for consumers' needs and wants as well as the heart to meet these needs.

This book was developed with the concept of acquiring Natural Languages and the bilingual opportunities for Deaf children (American Sign Language and English in its written form). There is a growing pedagogical awareness that the equal application of two natural languages in educational settings as well as in homes is necessary to promote a bilingual environment for Deaf children and their families. While the field is growing in this direction, the lack of materials to meet these needs remains tremendous. This book is the first step in achieving our long-term goal to fill this gap.

The illustrative format of this book was designed to promote the acquisition of ASL and English independently yet simultaneously. Signs are linked to the illustrations as are English words; signs and

English words are not linked to each other. For example, the sign RUN in this book (Chapter 1) means running with legs. The English homonym "run" has numerous meanings, such as a "run" in one's stocking and to "run" for office. Therefore, when learning the sign RUN it is important to remember that it corresponds to the illustration and not to the English word. ASL also has many homonyms (one sign which has several meanings), however, they are not included in this text.

The book is divided into six chapters and includes number signs and the manual alphabet. There is an index of ASL handshapes which may serve as a guide when looking for various signs, although the listing utilizes English words. The handshapes included in this text are based on the phonemes in ASL, as opposed to the manual representation of the English alphabet.

The first chapter "Verbs", includes both action and non-action verbs. They are presented in an amusing manner by children, clowns and bears. The focus of the second chapter is on Adjectives including feelings and opposites. The section on opposites is not presented in alphabetical order but rather presented with a sign, English word, and an illustration on one page with its opposite on the adjacent page. Chapter Three focuses on a broad range of nouns: People, Families, Transportation, Houses, Safety, Toys, Animals and Plants. Chapter Four is Pronouns. In ASL, the eye gaze is crucial when using pronouns. You are therefore encouraged to look carefully at the eye gazes when studying this chapter. Chapters Five and Six are Number Signs & American Manual Alphabet which are also essential to learning ASL.

As the sun sets, we present this book as one of the ideas that sprung out of the house by the sea. We look forward to Dawn because DawnSignPress has a whole new day ahead, down at the press.

Signing On,

Ben

Joe

Verbs

cook

cry

dance

Verbs

act

build

catch

chase

clean

climb

Verbs

cook

cry

dance

Verbs

dig

dive

draw

dream

drink

drive

Verbs

eat

fall

feed

Verbs

feel

find

fish

Verbs

fly

fly-a-kite

give

9

Verbs

help

hide

hit (with bat)

10

ice skate

jump

kiss

knit

laugh

lose

FRUIT

Verbs

love

make

paint

pet

plant

play

Verbs

pull

push

put

read

ride-bike

roll

Verbs

roller skate

row

run

Verbs

search

see

sew

Verbs

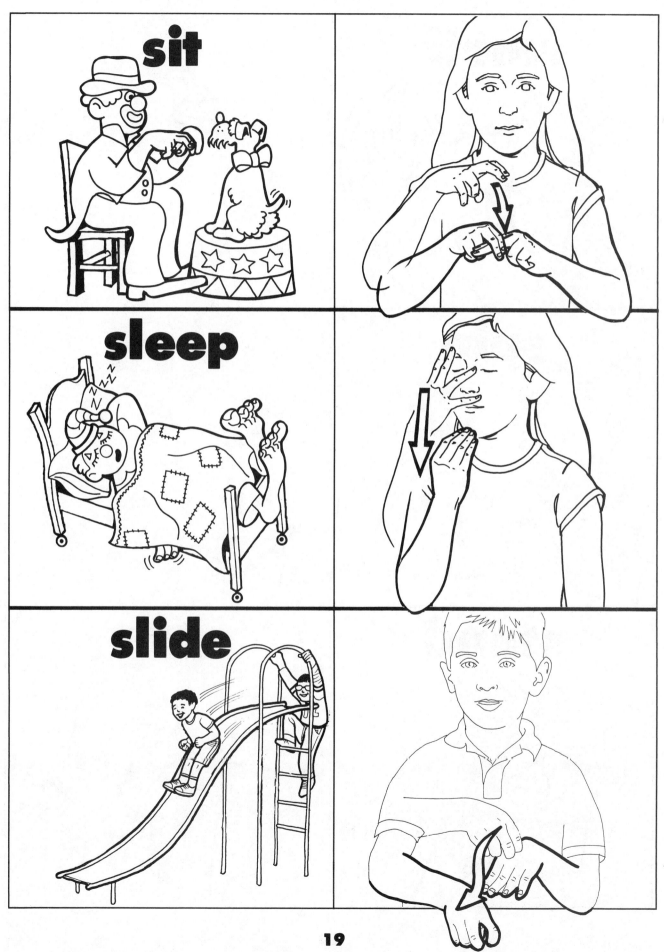

sit

sleep

slide

smell

spin

stand

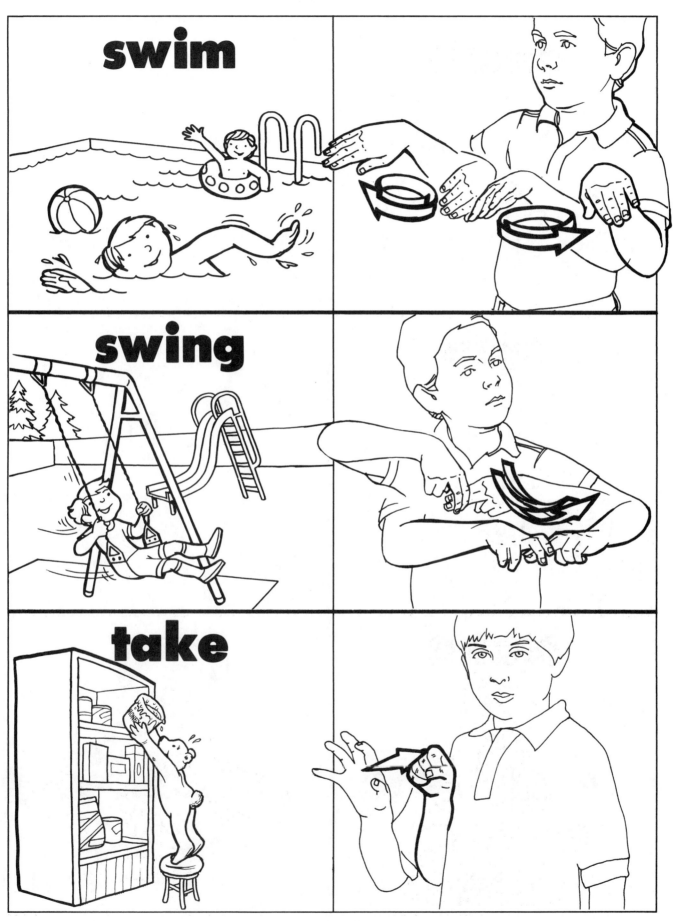

swim

swing

take

Verbs

talk (chat)

taste

HONEY

throw

2

Verbs

tip toe

trade

walk

Verbs

wash dishes

watch

MY HORSE IS FAST

write

Adjectives

bored

brave

embarrassed

excited

foolish

friendly

frustrated

happy

hurt (feelings)

jealous

lonely

mad

mean

nervous

nice

proud

sad

scared

shy

silly

snob

surprise

thirsty

tired

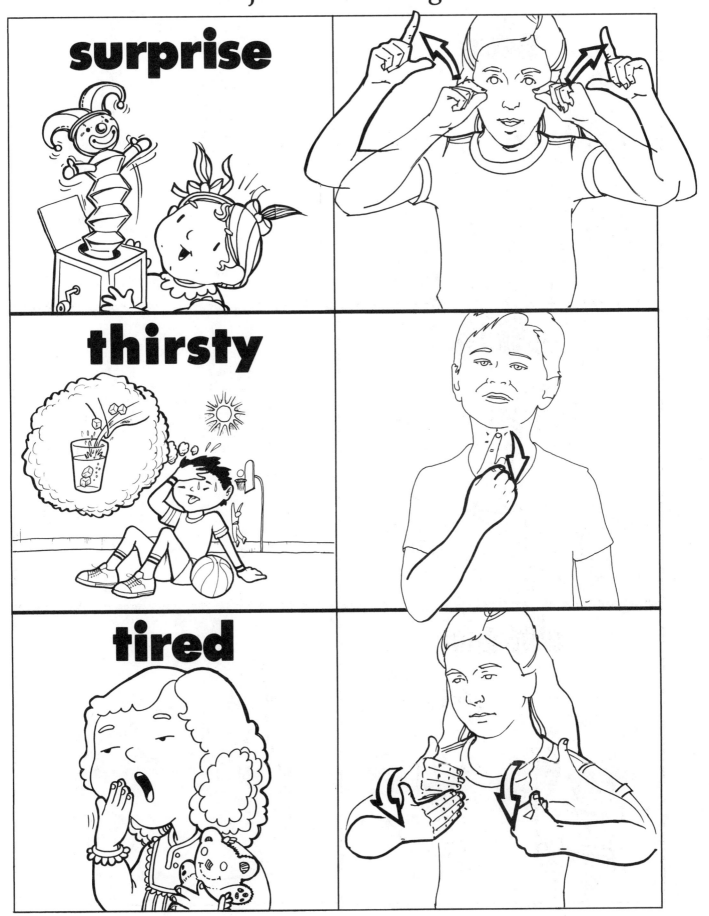

big

bright

clean

small

dark

dirty

cold

difficult

fat

hot

easy

thin

full

heavy

high

hungry

light

in

many

near

out

few

far

open

pretty

real

closed

ugly

fake

short

sick

soft

tall

well

hard

up

wet

young

down

dry

old

Nouns

horse

lion

monkey

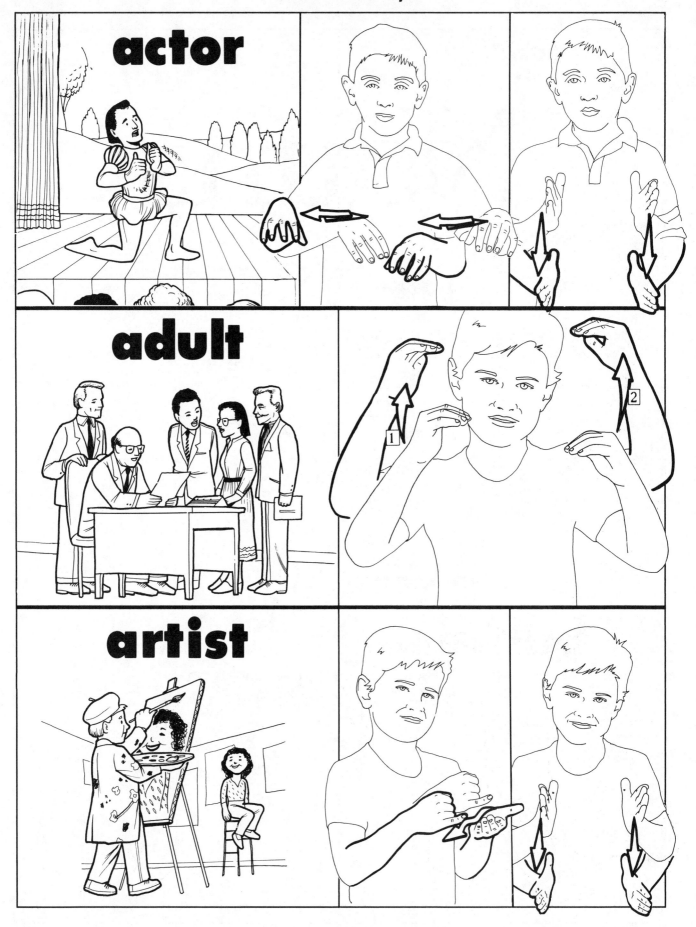

actor

adult

artist

baby

babysitter

barber

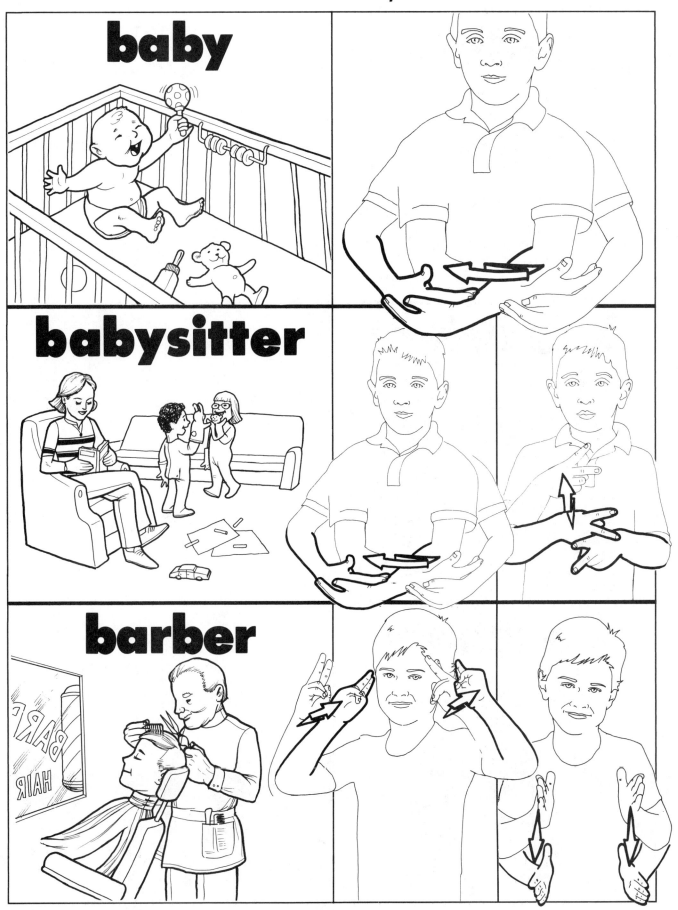

boy

bus driver

carpenter

chef

children

clown

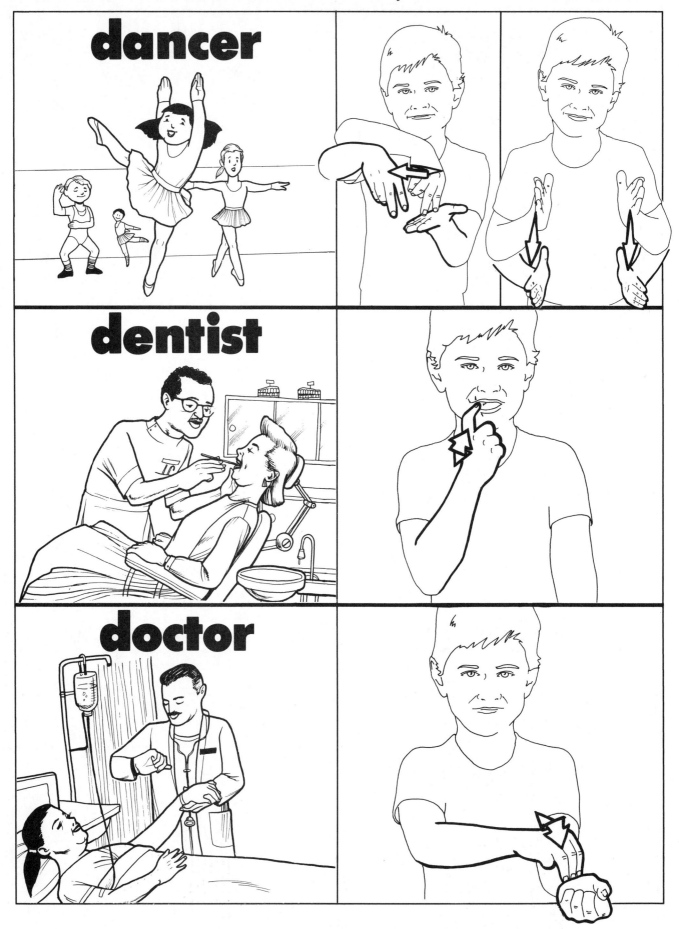

dancer

dentist

doctor

farmer

firefighter

fisherman

friend

girl

librarian

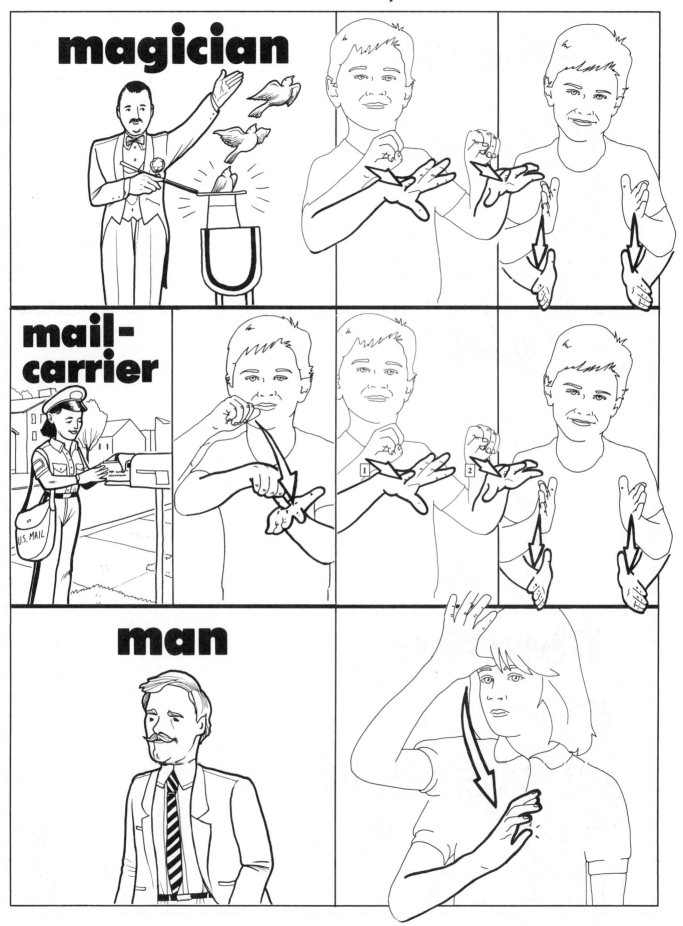

magician

mail-carrier

man

mechanic

neighbor

nurse

painter

people

pilot

police

salesperson

scientist

veterinarian

waitress

woman

family

aunt

brother

father

grandmother

grandfather

mother

parents

sister

uncle

airplane

bicycle

boat

bus

car

helicopter

motorcycle

rocket

subway

train

truck

transportation

basement

bathroom

bathtub

bed

bedroom

chair

curtain

door

dresser

dryer

garage

house

kitchen

lamp

living room

microwave oven

picture

refrigerator

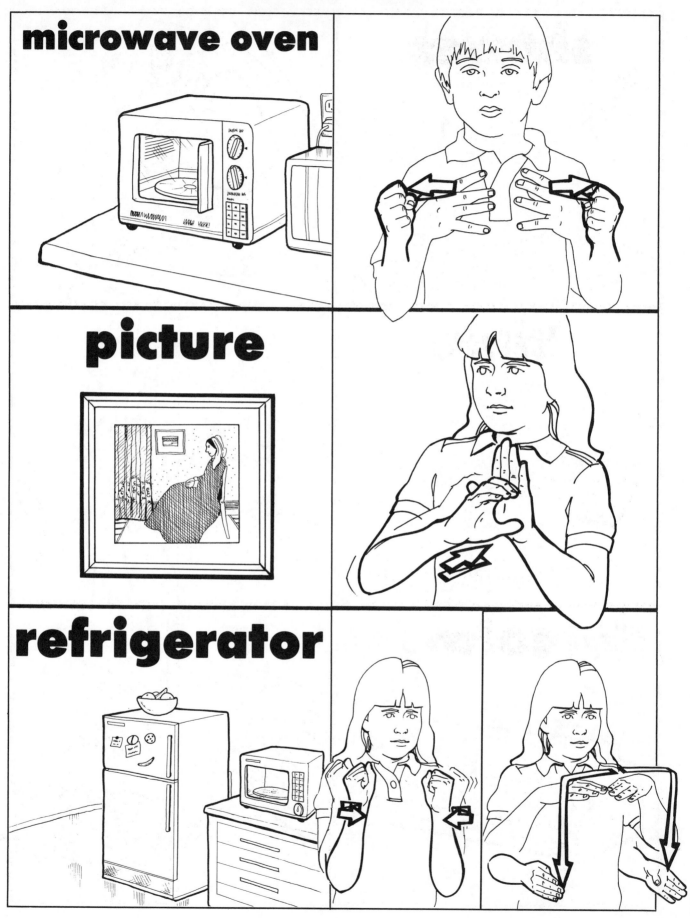

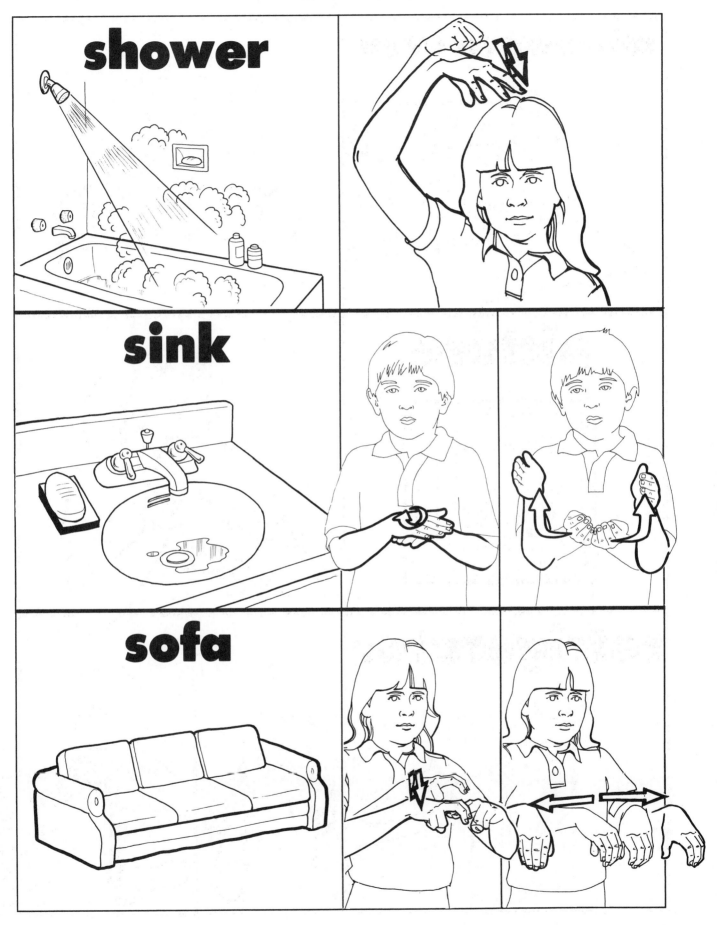

shower

sink

sofa

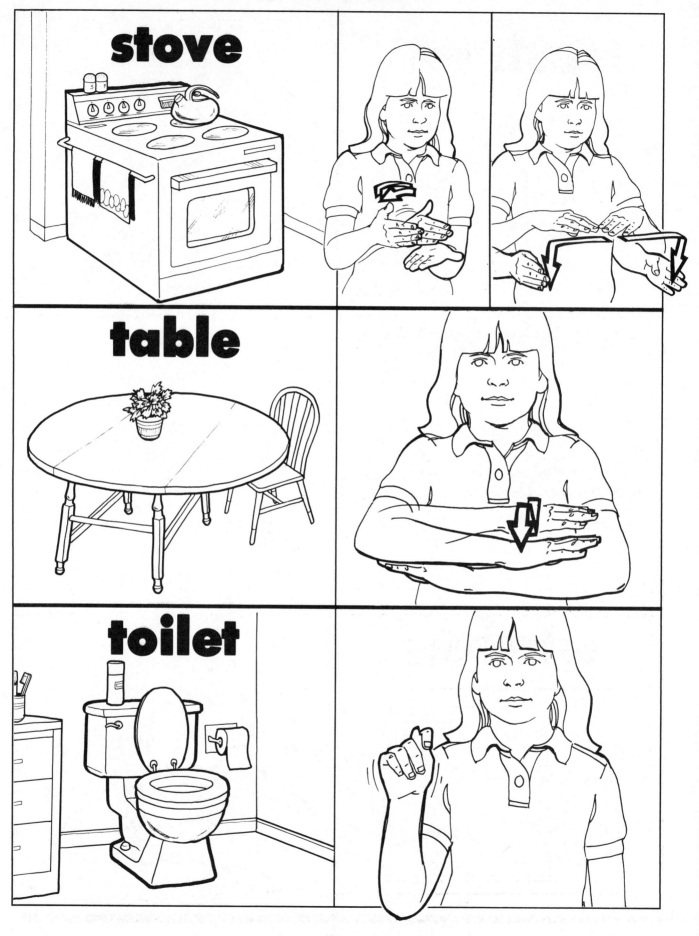

stove

table

toilet

trash can

washing machine

window

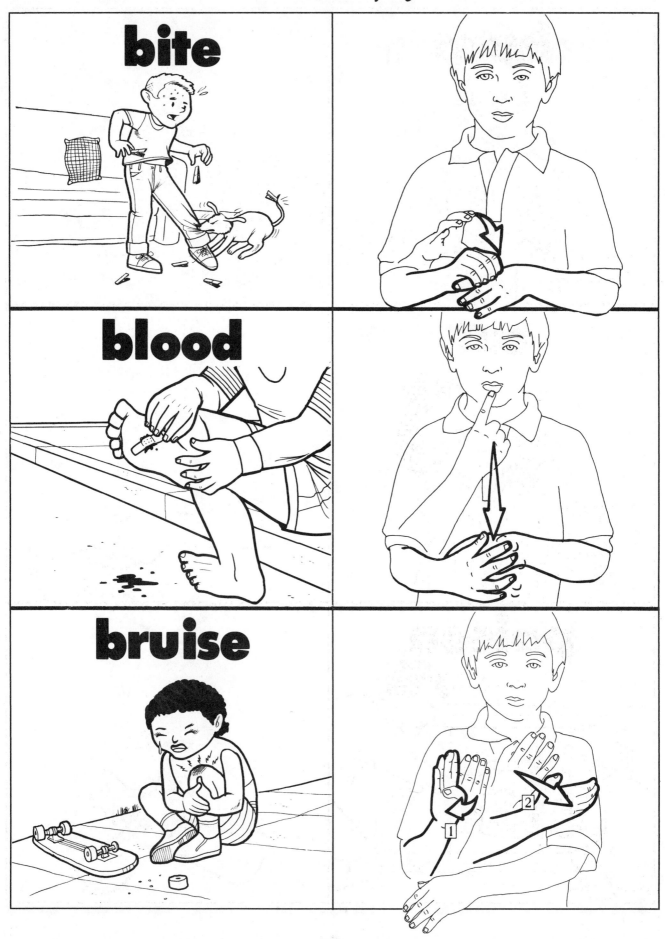

bite

blood

bruise

shock

sting

ball

crayon

doll

game

kite

puppet

rocking horse

sandbox

see-saw

skateboard

sled

toys

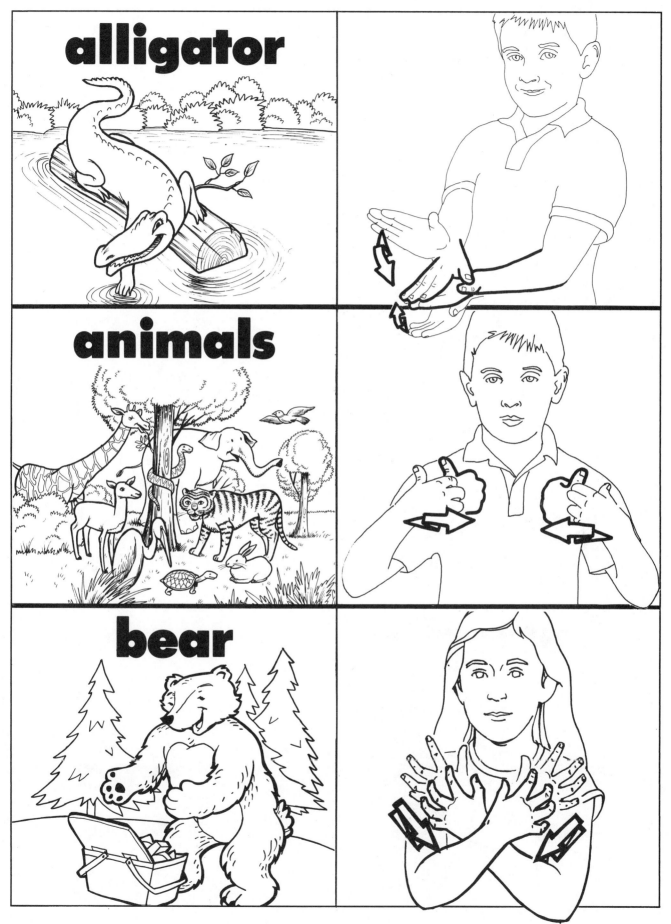

alligator

animals

bear

bee

bird

butterfly

cat

chicken

cow

deer

dinosaur

dog

duck

elephant

fish

fox

frog

giraffe

horse

lion

monkey

mouse

pig

rabbit

raccoon

sheep

skunk

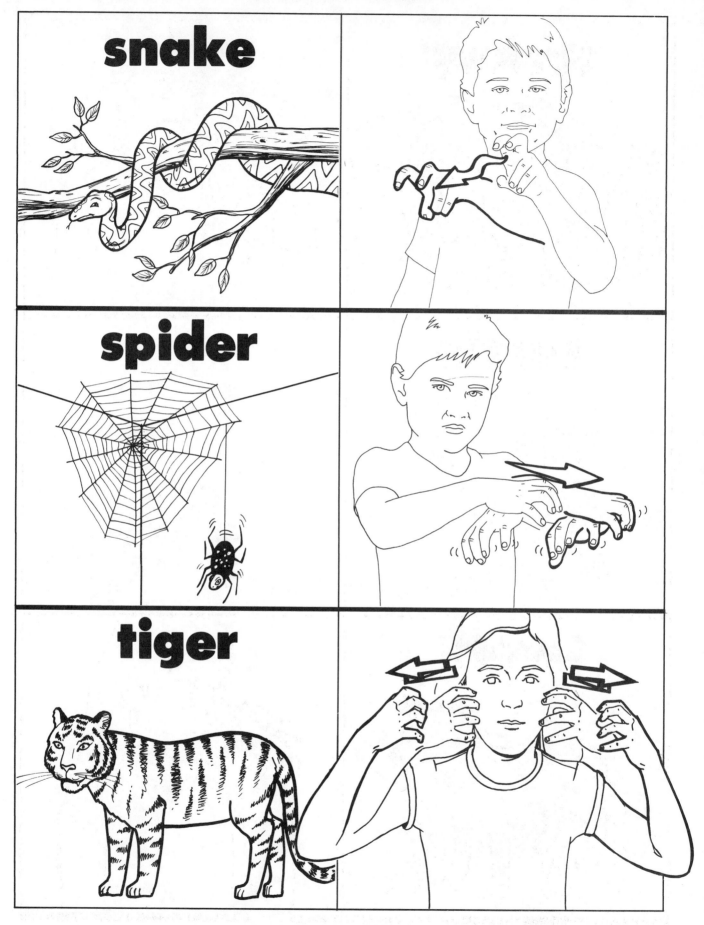

snake

spider

tiger

turkey

turtle

wolf

flower

grass

plant

tree

Pronouns

you

you-all

your (yours)

Pronouns

it

my (mine)

our (ours)

their (theirs)

they

we / us

you

you-all

your (yours)

Number Signs

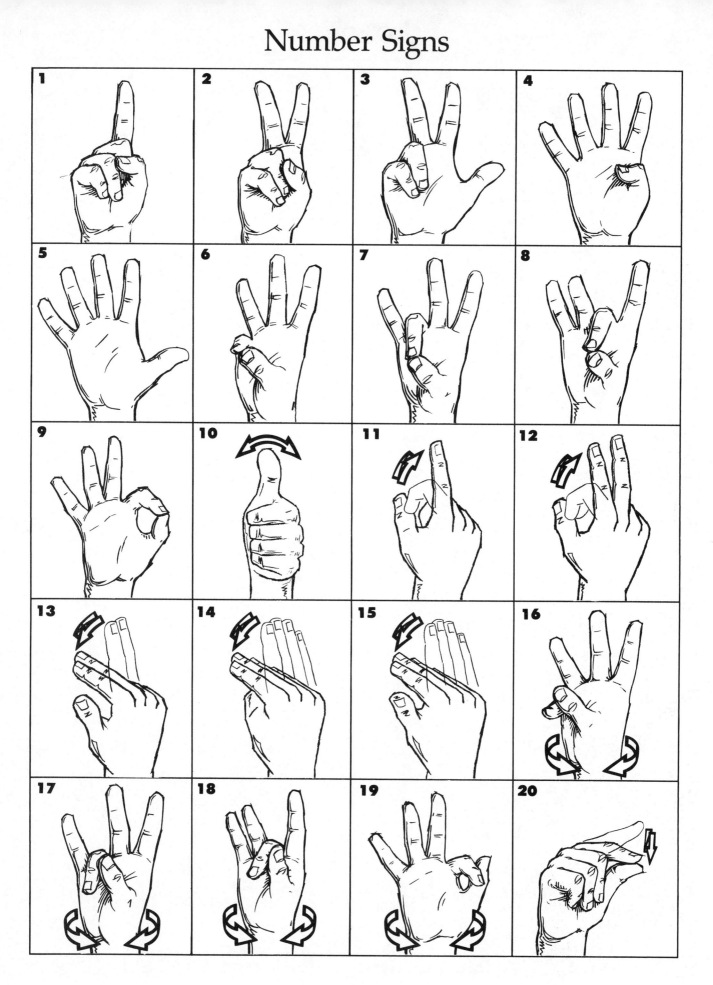

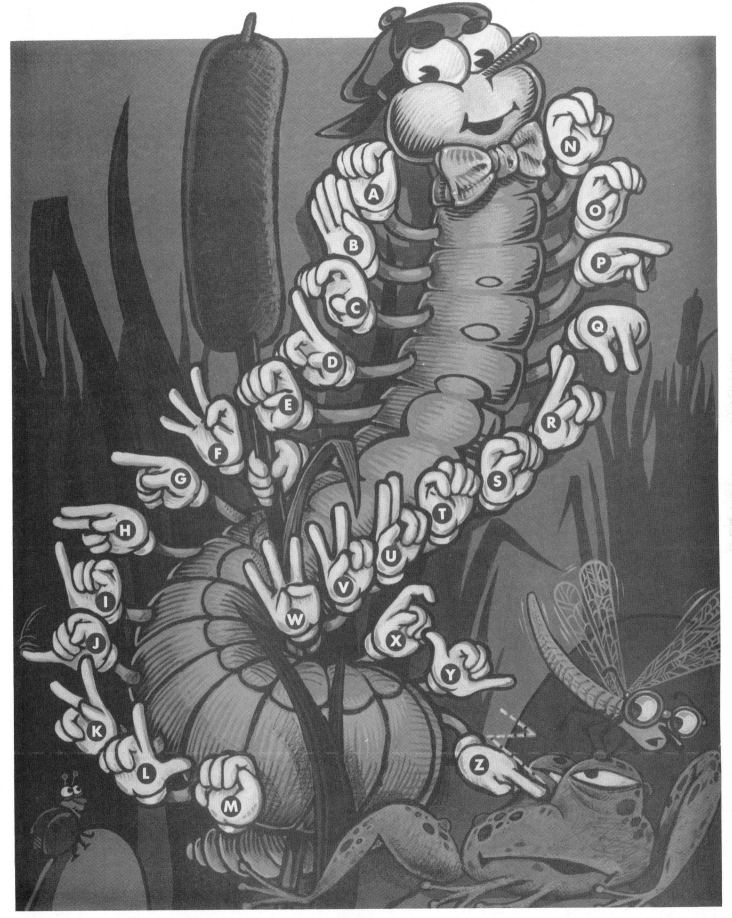

AUNT p. 64	TURTLE p. 97	
BATHTUB p. 71	WASH p. 24	
BROTHER p. 64		
FEW p. 41		
HIDE p. 10		
PLANT p. 14		
SISTER p. 66		
SPIN p. 20		

BICYCLE p. 67	DRIVE p. 6	
BRAVE p. 26	FROG p. 92	
BUSDRIVER p. 52	LOVE p. 13	
CAR p. 68	MAGICIAN p. 57	
CARPENTER p. 52	MAILCARRIER p. 57	
CATCH p. 2	MAKE p. 13	
COLD p. 36	MANY p. 40	
DRESSER p. 73	MEAN p. 30	

MICROWAVE OVEN p. 76	SCARED p. 31	
MOTORCYCLE p. 69	SHOWER p. 77	
OLD p. 47	SLED p. 86	
PULL p. 15	TAKE p. 21	
REFRIGERATOR p. 76	THROW p. 22	
RIDE p. 16	TRUCK p. 70	
ROW p. 17	WELL p. 45	

CRY p. 4	UGLY p. 43
DENTIST p. 54	
DOLL p. 83	
DREAM p. 6	
DRY p. 47	
DRYER p. 74	
FRIEND p. 56	
ICE SKATE p. 11	

BATHTUB p. 71	HE/SHE p. 102	LONELY p. 29	TALL p. 45	US p. 104
BLOOD p. 80	HIM/HER p. 102	ME p. 102	THEM p. 104	WE p. 104
BORED p. 26	HIT p. 10	MECHANIC p. 58	THEY p. 104	YOU p. 105
CRY p. 4	HURT p. 28	MOUSE p. 94	THIRSTY p. 33	YOU ALL p. 105
CUT p. 81	IT p. 103	REAL p. 42	TIP TOE p. 23	
DOWN p. 47	I p. 102	ROLL p. 16	TRASH CAN p. 79	
DREAM p. 6	KNIT p. 12	SNOB p. 32	UGLY p. 43	
FAKE p. 43	LAUGH p. 12	SUBWAY p. 69	UP p. 46	

BARBER p. 51	SLIDE p. 19	BABYSITTER p. 51	RACCOON p. 95
CHAIR p. 72	SOFA p. 77	BARBER p. 51	READ p. 16
DIVE p. 5	SWING p. 21	DANCE p. 4	SEE p. 18
HIGH p. 38	THIEF p. 61	DANCER p. 54	STAND p. 20
NURSE p. 58	TRAIN p. 70	FALL p. 7	VETERINARIAN p. 62
RABBIT p. 94	TRANSPORTATION p. 70	FROG p. 92	WATCH p. 24
RACCOON p. 95	UNCLE p. 66	JUMP p. 11	
SIT p. 19		MECHANIC p. 58	

DIFFICULT p. 36	SNAKE p. 96
HARD p. 45	
JUMP p. 11	
POISON p. 81	
ROLLERSKATE p. 17	
SEESAW p. 86	
SKATEBOARD p. 86	
SLIDE p. 19	

ARTIST p. 50
DRAW p. 5
JEALOUS p. 29

BRUISE p. 80	FIREFIGHTER p. 55
BUS DRIVER p. 52	FRUSTRATED p. 28
BEE p. 88	FULL p. 38
BURN p. 81	HOUSE p. 74
BUS p. 68	OPEN p. 42
CLOSED p. 43	REFRIGERATOR p. 76
DOOR p. 73	STOVE p. 78
ELEPHANT p. 91	WINDOW p. 70

CURTAIN p. 73
FEW p. 41

FAMILY p. 63
FOX p. 92
PUPPET p. 84

BIRD p. 88
CHICKEN p. 89
SURPRISE p. 33
THIN p. 37
TURKEY p. 97

BOY p. 52	KISS p. 11	SANDBOX p. 85
BRIGHT p. 34	LOSE p. 12	SLEEP p. 19
DINOSAUR p. 90	OUT p. 41	SOFT p. 44
EAT p. 7	PLANT p. 14	TEACHER p. 61
FEED p. 7	PLANT p. 99	WET p. 46
FLOWER p. 98	PRETTY p. 42	WOLF p. 97
GIVE p. 9	PUT p. 15	
IN p. 40	SALESPERSON p. 60	

BASEMENT p. 71
CHASE p. 3
FAR p. 41
GAME p. 84
GIRL p. 56
HELP p. 10
MAILCARRIER p. 57
PROUD p. 31

SCIENTIST p. 60

COW p. 89
FOOLISH p. 27
PLAY p. 14
SILLY p. 32
TOYS p. 86

ACTOR p. 50
ALLIGATOR p. 87
ARTIST p. 50
BARBER p. 51
BASEMENT p. 71
BED p. 72
BEDROOM p. 72
BITE p. 80
BUSDRIVER p. 52
CARPENTER p. 52
CHEF p. 53
CHICKEN p. 89
CHILDREN p. 53
CLEAN p. 3
CLEAN p. 34
COOK p. 4

DANCE p. 4
DANCER p. 54
DARK p. 35
DRAW p. 5
EASY p. 37
FALL p. 7
FARMER p. 55
FISH p. 91
FISHERMAN p. 55
FLY p. 9
GARAGE p. 74
HAPPY p. 28
HELP p. 10
HIS/HERS p. 102
JUMP p. 11
LIBRARIAN p. 56

LIVING ROOM p. 75
LOW p. 39
MAGICIAN p. 57
MAILCARRIER p. 57
MECHANIC p. 58
MINE p. 103
MY p. 103
NEAR p. 40
NICE p. 30
PAINT p. 13
PAINTER p. 59
PET p. 14
PICTURE p. 76
PIG p. 94
PILOT p. 59
PUSH p. 15

READ p. 16
ROCKET p. 69
ROCKINGHORSE p. 85
SALESPERSON p. 60
SANDBOX p. 85
SCIENTIST p. 60
SHORT p. 44
SINGER p. 61
SINK p. 77
SMELL p. 20
STAND p. 20
STOVE p. 78
SUBWAY p. 69
TABLE p. 78
TALL p. 45
TEACHER p. 61

THEIR p. 104
THEIRS p. 104
WAITRESS p. 62
WALK p. 23
WASH p. 24
YOUR p. 105
YOURS p. 105

BITE p. 80
BRUISE p. 80
DRINK p. 6
GIRAFFE p. 92
HUNGRY p. 39
IN p. 40
OLD p. 47
OUT p. 41

PICTURE p. 76
POLICE p. 60
SEARCH p. 18
SOFA p. 77

ACT p. 2
ACTOR p. 50
BALL p. 83
BEAR p. 87
BRAVE p. 26
CATCH p. 2
CLIMB p. 3
CLOWN p. 53

GRASS p. 98
HOT p. 37
LION p. 93
MAD p. 29
MEAN p. 30
MONKEY p. 93
SHOCK p. 82
SPIDER p. 96

TAKE p. 21
TIGER p. 96
WASHING
   MACHINE p. 79
WELL p. 45

EXCITED p. 27
FEEL p. 8
LIGHT p. 39
SICK p. 44
TASTE p. 22

BLOOD p. 80
BRIGHT p. 34
BUTTERFLY p. 88
CRAYON p. 83
DEER p. 90
DIRTY p. 36
EMBARRASSED p. 26
FARMER p. 55

FAT p. 36
FATHER p. 64
FRIENDLY p. 27
GRANDFATHER p. 65
GRANDMOTHER p. 65
HELICOPTER p. 68
LIVING ROOM p. 75
LOSE p. 12

MAGICIAN p. 57
MAN p. 57
MANY p. 40
MOTHER p. 65
NERVOUS p. 30
PARENTS p. 66
SAD p. 31
SCARED p. 31

TALK p. 22
TREE p. 99
WET p. 46
WOMAN p. 62

ADULT p. 50
ANIMALS p. 87
BABY p. 51
BABYSITTER p. 51
BOAT p. 67
BUILD p. 2
DIG p. 5
DOCTOR p. 54

HEAVY p. 38
HIDE p. 10
OUR p. 103
OURS p. 103
SHY p. 32
SINK p. 77
SMALL p. 35
SWIM p. 21

TIRED p. 33
TURTLE p. 97
YOUNG p. 46

MAILCARRIER p. 57
MICROWAVE
   OVEN p. 76
OUT p. 41
PLANT p. 99
PRETTY p. 42
SHOWER p. 77
SLEEP p. 19

SOFT p. 44
WOLF p. 97

*

*

BATHROOM p. 71
TOILET p. 78

CRAYON p. 83
STING p. 82
WRITE p. 24

*

* NOTE: SIGN NOT IN BOOK

ASL Index

	DUCK p. 91	*		LAMP p. 75
*	AIRPLANE p. 67 PILOT p. 59	*		
	GARAGE p. 74 HELICOPTER p. 68 ROCKING HORSE p. 85 THROW p. 22	*		BIG p. 34 RUN p. 17
	BROTHER p. 64 LIBRARIAN p. 56 SISTER p. 66 SURPRISE p. 33 RUN p. 17		DOG p. 90	PEOPLE p. 59 SHEEP p. 95 SKUNK p. 95
	ROCKET p. 69		FISH p. 8 FISHERMAN p. 55 FLY-A-KITE p. 9 KITE p. 84 SPIN p. 20 TRADE p. 23	CAT p. 89 FIND p. 8 SEW p. 18
	BOY p. 52		HORSE p. 93 ROCKINGHORSE p. 85	

* NOTE: SIGN NOT IN BOOK

Index

A

ACT — p. 2
ACTOR — p. 50
ADULT — p. 50
AIRPLANE — p. 67
ALLIGATOR — p. 87
ANIMALS — p. 87
ARTIST — p. 50
AUNT — p. 64

B

BABY — p. 51
BABYSITTER — p. 51
BALL — p. 83
BARBER — p. 51
BASEMENT — p. 71
BATHROOM — p. 71
BATHTUB — p. 71
BEAR — p. 87
BED — p. 72
BEDROOM — p. 72
BEE — p. 88
BICYCLE — p. 67
BIG — p. 34
BIRD — p. 88
BITE — p. 80
BLOOD — p. 80
BOAT — p. 67
BORED — p. 26
BOY — p. 52
BRAVE — p. 26
BRIGHT — p. 34
BROTHER — p. 64
BRUISE — p. 80
BUILD — p. 2
BURN — p. 81
BUS — p. 68
BUSDRIVER — p. 52
BUTTERFLY — p. 88

C

CAR — p. 68
CARPENTER — p. 52
CAT — p. 89
CATCH — p. 2
CHAIR — p. 72
CHASE — p. 3
CHEF — p. 53
CHICKEN — p. 89
CHILDREN — p. 53
CLEAN — p. 3, 34
CLIMB — p. 3
CLOSED — p. 43
CLOWN — p. 53
COLD — p. 36
COOK — p. 4
COW — p. 89
CRAYON — p. 83
CRY — p. 4
CURTAIN — p. 73
CUT — p. 81

D

DANCE — p. 4
DANCER — p. 54
DARK — p. 35
DEER — p. 90
DENTIST — p. 54
DIFFICULT — p. 36
DIG — p. 5

DINOSAUR — p. 90
DIRTY — p. 35
DIVE — p. 5
DOCTOR — p. 54
DOG — p. 90
DOLL — p. 83
DOOR — p. 73
DOWN — p. 47
DRAW — p. 5
DREAM — p. 6
DRESSER — p. 73
DRINK — p. 6
DRIVE — p. 6
DRY — p. 47
DRYER — p. 74
DUCK — p. 91

E

EASY — p. 37
EAT — p. 7
ELEPHANT — p. 91
EMBARRASSED — p. 26
EXCITED — p. 27

F

FAKE — p. 43
FALL — p. 7
FAMILY — p. 63
FAR — p. 41
FARMER — p. 55
FAT — p. 36
FATHER — p. 64
FEED — p. 7
FEEL — p. 8
FEW — p. 41
FIND — p. 8
FIREFIGHTER — p. 55
FISH — p. 8, 91
FISHERMAN — p. 55
FLOWER — p. 98
FLY — p. 9
FLY-A-KITE — p. 9
FOOLISH — p. 27
FOX — p. 92
FRIEND — p. 56
FRIENDLY — p. 27
FROG — p. 92
FRUSTRATED — p. 28
FULL — p. 38

G

GAME — p. 84
GARAGE — p. 74
GIRAFFE — p. 92
GIRL — p. 56
GIVE — p. 9
GRANDFATHER — p. 65
GRANDMOTHER — p. 65
GRASS — p. 98

H

HAPPY — p. 28
HARD — p. 45
HE — p. 102
HEAVY — p. 38
HELICOPTER — p. 68
HELP — p. 10
HER — p. 102
HERS — p. 102
HIDE — p. 10

HIGH — p. 38
HIM — p. 102
HIS — p. 102
HIT — p. 10
HORSE — p. 93
HOT — p. 37
HOUSE — p. 74
HUNGRY — p. 39
HURT — p. 28

I

I — p. 102
ICE SKATE — p. 11
IN — p. 40
IT — p. 103

J

JEALOUS — p. 29
JUMP — p. 11

K

KISS — p. 11
KITCHEN — p. 75
KITE — p. 84
KNIT — p. 12

L

LAMP — p. 75
LAUGH — p. 12
LIBRARIAN — p. 56
LIGHT — p. 39
LION — p. 93
LIVING ROOM — p. 75
LONELY — p. 29
LOSE — p. 12
LOVE — p. 13
LOW — p. 39

M

MAD — p. 29
MAGICIAN — p. 57
MAILCARRIER — p. 57
MAKE — p. 13
MAN — p. 57
MANY — p. 40
ME — p. 102
MEAN — p. 30
MECHANIC — p. 58
MICROWAVE OVEN — p. 76
MINE — p. 103
MONKEY — p. 93
MOTHER — p. 65
MOTORCYCLE — p. 69
MOUSE — p. 94
MY — p. 103

N

NEAR — p. 40
NEIGHBOR — p. 58
NERVOUS — p. 30
NICE — p. 30
NURSE — p. 58

O

OLD — p. 47
OPEN — p. 42
OUR — p. 103
OURS — p. 103
OUT — p. 41

P

PAINT — p. 13
PAINTER — p. 59
PARENTS — p. 66
PEOPLE — p. 59
PET — p. 14
PICTURE — p. 76
PIG — p. 94
PILOT — p. 59
PLANT — p. 14, 99
PLAY — p. 14
POISON — p. 81
POLICE — p. 60
PRETTY — p. 42
PROUD — p. 31
PULL — p. 15
PUPPET — p. 84
PUSH — p. 15
PUT — p. 15

R

RABBIT — p. 94
RACCOON — p. 95
READ — p. 16
REAL — p. 42
REFRIGERATOR — p. 76
RIDE — p. 16
ROCKET — p. 69
ROCKINGHORSE — p. 85
ROLL — p. 16
ROLLERSKATE — p. 17
ROW — p. 17
RUN — p. 17

S

SAD — p. 31
SALESPERSON — p. 60
SANDBOX — p. 85
SCARED — p. 31
SCIENTIST — p. 60
SEARCH — p. 18
SEE — p. 18
SEESAW — p. 85
SEW — p. 18
SHE — p. 102
SHEEP — p. 95
SHOCK — p. 82
SHORT — p. 44
SHOWER — p. 77
SHY — p. 32
SICK — p. 44
SILLY — p. 32
SINGER — p. 61
SINK — p. 77
SISTER — p. 66
SIT — p. 19
SKATEBOARD — p. 86
SKUNK — p. 95
SLED — p. 86
SLEEP — p. 19
SLIDE — p. 19
SMALL — p. 35
SMELL — p. 20
SNAKE — p. 96
SNOB — p. 32
SOFA — p. 77
SOFT — p. 44
SPIDER — p. 96
SPIN — p. 20
STAND — p. 20

STING — p. 82
STOVE — p. 78
SUBWAY — p. 69
SURPRISE — p. 33
SWIM — p. 21
SWING — p. 21

T

TABLE — p. 78
TAKE — p. 21
TALK — p. 22
TALL — p. 45
TASTE — p. 22
TEACHER — p. 61
THEIR — p. 104
THEIRS — p. 104
THEM — p. 104
THEY — p. 104
THIEF — p. 61
THIN — p. 37
THIRSTY — p. 33
THROW — p. 22
TIGER — p. 96
TIP TOE — p. 23
TIRED — p. 33
TOILET — p. 78
TOYS — p. 86
TRADE — p. 23
TRAIN — p. 70
TRANSPORTATION — p. 70
TRASH CAN — p. 79
TREE — p. 99
TRUCK — p. 70
TURKEY — p. 97
TURTLE — p. 97

U

UGLY — p. 43
UNCLE — p. 66
UP — p. 46
US — p. 104

V

VETERINARIAN — p. 62

W

WAITRESS — p. 62
WALK — p. 23
WASH — p. 24
WASH MACHINE — p. 79
WATCH — p. 24
WE — p. 104
WELL — p. 45
WET — p. 46
WINDOW — p. 70
WOLF — p. 97
WOMAN — p. 62
WRITE — p. 24

Y

YOUNG — p. 46
YOU — p. 105
YOU ALL — p. 105
YOUR — p. 105
YOURS — p. 105

Indíce

A

ACT — ACTUAR p. 2
ACTOR — ACTOR p. 50
ADULT — ADULTO p. 50
AIRPLANE — AVIÓN p. 67
ALLIGATOR — LAGARTO p. 87
ANIMALS — ANIMALES p. 87
ARTIST — ARTISTA p. 50
AUNT — TÍA p. 64

B

BABY — BEBÉ p. 51
BABYSITTER — NIÑERA p. 51
BALL — PELOTA p. 83
BARBER — BARBERO p. 51
BASEMENT — SÓTANO p. 47
BATHROOM — BAÑO p. 71
BATHTUB — BAÑERA p. 71
BEAR — OSO p. 87
BED — CAMA p. 72
BEDROOM — RECÁMARA p. 72
BEE — ABEJA p. 88
BICYCLE — BICICLETA p. 67
BIG — GRANDE p. 34
BIRD — PÁJARO p. 88
BITE — MORDER p. 80
BLOOD — SANGRE p. 80
BOAT — LANCHA p. 67
BORED — ABURRIDO p. 26
BOY — MUCHACHO p. 52
BRAVE — VALIENTE p. 26
BRIGHT — BRILLANTE p. 34
BROTHER — HERMANO p. 64
BRUISE — RASPÓN p. 80
BUILD — CONSTRUIR p. 2
BURN — QUEMADA p. 81
BUS — AUTOBÚS p. 68
BUSDRIVER — CHÓFER p. 52
BUTTERFLY — MARIPOSA p. 88

C

CAR — CARRO p. 68
CARPENTER — CARPINTERO p. 52
CAT — GATO p. 89
CATCH — ATRAPAR p. 2
CHAIR — SILLA p. 72
CHASE — PERSEGUIR p. 3
CHEF — CHEF p. 53
CHICKEN — POLLO p. 89
CHILDREN — NIÑOS p. 53
CLEAN — LIMPIO p. 3, 34
CLIMB — TREPAR p. 3
CLOSED — CERRADO p. 43
CLOWN — PAYASO p. 53
COLD — FRIO p. 36
COOK — COCINERO p. 36
COW — VACA p. 89
CRAYON — CRAYÓN p. 83
CRY — LLORAR p. 4
CURTAIN — CORTINA p. 73
CUT — CORTAR p. 81

D

DANCE — BAILAR p. 4
DANCER — BAILARIN p. 54
DARK — OSCURO p. 35
DEER — VENADO p. 90
DENTIST — DENTISTA p. 54
DIFFICULT — DIFÍCIL p. 36
DIG — EXCAVAR p. 5
DINOSAUR — DINOSAURIO p. 90
DIRTY — SUCIO p. 35
DIVE — BUCEAR p. 5
DOCTOR — DOCTOR p. 54

DOG — PERRO p. 90
DOLL — MUÑECA p. 83
DOOR — PUERTA p. 73
DOWN — ABAJO p. 47
DRAW — DIBUJAR p. 5
DREAM — SOÑAR p. 6
DRESSER — CÓMODA p. 73
DRINK — BEBER p. 6
DRIVE — MANEJAR p. 6
DRY — SECAR p. 47
DRYER — SECADORA p. 74
DUCK — PATO p. 91

E

EASY — FÁCIL p. 37
EAT — COMER p. 7
ELEPHANT — ELEFANTE p. 91
EMBARRASSED — AVERGONZADO p. 26
EXCITED — EXCITADO p. 27

F

FAKE — FALSO p. 43
FALL — OTOÑO p. 7
FAMILY — FAMILIA p. 63
FAR — LEJOS p. 41
FARMER — AGRICULTOR p. 55
FAT — GORDO p. 36
FATHER — PADRE p. 64
FEED — ALIMENTAR p. 7
FEEL — SENTIR p. 8
FEW — POCOS p. 41
FIND — ENCONTRAR p. 8
FIREFIGHTER — BOMBERO p. 55
FISH — PEZ p. 8, 91
FISHERMAN — PESCADOR p. 55
FLOWER — FLOR p. 98
FLY — VOLAR p. 9
FLY-A-KITE — VOLAR LA COMETA p. 9
FOOLISH — TONTO p. 27
FOX — ZORRO p. 92
FRIEND — AMIGO p. 56
FRIENDLY — AMISTOSO p. 27
FROG — RANA p. 92
FRUSTRATED — FRUSTRADO p. 28
FULL — LLENO p. 38

G

GAME — JUEGO p. 84
GARAGE — GARAJE p. 74
GIRAFFE — JIRAFA p. 92
GIRL — MUCHACHA p. 56
GIVE — DAR p. 9
GRANDFATHER — ABUELO p. 65
GRANDMOTHER — ABUELA p. 65
GRASS — PASTO p. 98

H

HAPPY — FELIZ p. 28
HARD — DURO p. 45
HE — ÉL p. 102
HEAVY — PESADO p. 38
HELICOPTER — HELICÓPTERO p. 68
HELP — AYUDA p. 10
HER — ELLA (posesivo, objetivo) p. 102
HERS — PERTENECIENTE A ELLA p. 102
HIDE — ESCONDER p. 10
HIGH — ALTO p. 38
HIM — ÉL (posesivo, objetivo) p. 102

HIS — PERTENECIENTE A ÉL p. 102
HIT — GOLPEAR p. 10
HORSE — CABALLO p. 93
HOT — CALIENTE p. 37
HOUSE — CASA p. 74
HUNGRY — HAMBRIENTO p. 39
HURT — GOLPEADO p. 28

I

I — YO p. 102
ICE SKATE — PATINAJE SOBRE EL HIELO p. 11
IN — EN p. 40
IT — PRONOMBRE PARA COSAS p. 103

J

JEALOUS — CELOSO p. 29
JUMP — SALTAR p. 11

K

KISS — BESAR p. 11
KITCHEN — COCINA p. 75
KITE — COMETA p. 84
KNIT — TEJER p. 12

L

LAMP — LÁMPARA p. 75
LAUGH — REÍR p. 12
LIBRARIAN — BIBLOTECARIA p. 56
LIGHT — LIVIANO p. 39
LION — LEÓN p. 93
LIVING ROOM — SALA DE ESTAR p. 75
LONELY — SOLITARIO p. 29
LOSE — PERDER p. 12
LOVE — AMAR p. 13
LOW — BAJO p. 39

M

MAD — LOCO p. 29
MAGICIAN — MAGO p. 57
MAILCARRIER — CARTERO p. 57
MAKE — HACER p. 13
MAN — HOMBRE p. 57
MANY — MUCHOS p. 40
ME — YO (después de la preposición) p. 102
MEAN — MALVADO p. 30
MECHANIC — MECÁNICO p. 58
MICROWAVE OVEN — HORNO DE MICRONDAS p. 76
MINE — MIO p. 103
MONKEY — MONO p. 93
MOTHER — MADRE p. 65
MOTORCYCLE — MOTOCICLETA p. 69
MOUSE — RATÓN p. 94
MY — MIO (posed, pron., adj.) p. 103

N

NEAR — CERCA p. 40
NEIGHBOR — VECINO p. 58
NERVOUS — NERVIOSO p. 30
NICE — AGRADABLE p. 30
NURSE — ENFERMERA p. 58

O

OLD — VIEJO p. 47
OPEN — ABIERTO p. 42
OUR — NUESTRO p. 103

OURS — NUESTRO p. 103
OUT — AFUERA p. 41

P

PAINT — PINTURA p. 13
PAINTER — PINTOR p. 59
PARENTS — PADRES p. 66
PEOPLE — GENTE p. 59
PET — MASCOTA p. 14
PICTURE — RETRATO p. 76
PIG — CERDO p. 94
PILOT — PILOTO p. 59
PLANT — PLANTA p. 14, 99
PLAY — JUGAR p. 14
POISON — VENENO p. 81
POLICE — POLICÍA p. 60
PRETTY — BONITO p. 42
PROUD — ORGULLOSO p. 31
PULL — JALAR p. 15
PUPPET — TÍTERE p. 84
PUSH — EMPUJAR p. 15
PUT — PONER p. 15

R

RABBIT — CONEJO p. 94
RACCOON — MAPACHE p. 95
READ — LEER p. 16
REAL — REAL p. 42
REFRIGERATOR — REFRIGERADOR p. 76
RIDE — PASEARSE p. 16
ROCKET — COHETE p. 69
ROCKINGHORSE — CABALLO MECEDOR p. 85
ROLL — RODAR p. 16
ROLLERSKATE — PATINAR p. 17
ROW — REMAR p. 17
RUN — CORRER p. 17

S

SAD — TRISTE p. 31
SALESPERSON — VENDEDOR p. 60
SANDBOX — CAJA DE ARENA p. 85
SCARED — ASUSTADO p. 31
SCIENTIST — CIENTÍFICO p. 60
SEARCH — BUSCAR p. 18
SEE — VER p. 18
SEESAW — SUBE Y BAJA p. 85
SEW — COSER p. 18
SHE — ELLA p. 102
SHEEP — OVEJA p. 95
SHOCK — CHOQUE ELECTRICO p. 82
SHORT — PEQUEÑO p. 44
SHOWER — REGADERA p. 77
SHY — TÍMIDO p. 32
SICK — ENFERMO p. 44
SILLY — GRACIOSO p. 32
SINGER — CANTANTE p. 61
SINK — LAVABO p. 77
SISTER — HERMANA p. 66
SIT — SENTARSE p. 19
SKATEBOARD — PATINETA p. 86
SKUNK — ZORRILLO p. 95
SLED — TRINEO p. 86
SLEEP — DORMIR p. 19
SLIDE — RESBALARSE p. 19
SMALL — PEQUEÑO p. 35
SMELL — OLER p. 20
SNAKE — CULEBRA p. 96
SNOB — PEDANTE p. 32
SOFA — SOFÁ p. 77
SOFT — SUAVE p. 44
SPIDER — ARAÑA p. 96

SPIN — GIRAR p. 20
STAND — PARARSE p. 20
STING — PIQUETE p. 82
STOVE — ESTUFA p. 78
SUBWAY — TREN SUBTERRÁNEO p. 69
SURPRISE — SORPRESA p. 33
SWIM — NADAR p. 21
SWING — COLUMPIARSE p. 21

T

TABLE — MESA p. 78
TAKE — TOMAR p. 21
TALK — HABLAR p. 22
TALL — ALTO p. 45
TASTE — PROBAR p. 22
TEACHER — MAESTRO p. 61
THEIR — SUYO (de ellos) p. 104
THEIRS — SUYO p. 104
THEM — ELLOS p. 104
THEY — ELLOS p. 104
THIEF — LADRÓN p. 61
THIN — DELGADO p. 37
THIRSTY — SEDIENTO p. 33
THROW — LANZAR p. 22
TIGER — TIGRE p. 96
TIP TOE — DE PUNTILLAS p. 23
TIRED — CANSADO p. 33
TOILET — INODORO p. 78
TOYS — JUGUETES p. 86
TRADE — INTERCAMBIAR p. 23
TRAIN — TREN p. 70
TRANSPORTATION — TRANSPORTACIÓN p. 70
TRASH CAN — BOTE DE BASURA p. 79
TREE — ÁRBOL p. 99
TRUCK — CAMIÓN p. 70
TURKEY — PAVO p. 97
TURTLE — TORTUGA p. 97

U

UGLY — FEO p. 43
UNCLE — TÍO p. 66
UP — ARRIBA p. 46
US — NOSOTROS p. 104

V

VETERINARIAN — VETERINARO p. 62

W

WAITRESS — MESERA p. 62
WALK — CAMINAR p. 23
WASH — LAVAR p. 24
WASHING MACHINE — LAVADORA p. 79
WATCH — VER p. 24
WE — NOSOTROS p. 104
WELL — BIEN/BUENO p. 45
WET — MOJADO p. 46
WINDOW — VENTANA p. 70
WOLF — LOBO p. 97
WOMAN — MUJER p. 62
WRITE — ESCRIBIR p. 24

Y

YOUNG — JOVEN p. 46
YOU — TÚ (usted) p. 105
YOU ALL — TODOS USTEDES p. 105
YOUR — TUYO (de ustedes) p. 105
YOURS — TUYO (de ustedes) p. 105

លិបិក្រម

A
ACT សំដែង (ទ. ២)
ACTOR តួរងសំដែង (ទ. ៦០)
ADULT មនុស្សធំ (ទ. ៦០)
AIRPLANE យន្តហោះ (ទ. ១៣)
ALLIGATOR ក្រពើ (ទ. ៨៣)
ANIMALS សត្វៗ។ (ទ. ៨៣)
ARTIST សិល្បករ (ទ. ៦០)
AUNT ម្ដាយមីង (ទ. ១៤)

B
BABY កូនងែត ឬទារក (ទ. ៦១)
BABYSITTER អ្នកមើលកូន (ទ. ៦១)
BALL បាល់ (ទ. ៨៣)
BARBER ជាងកាត់សក់ (ទ. ៦១)
BASEMENT បន្ទប់ក្រោមដី (ទ. ៧៩)
BATHROOM បន្ទប់ទឹក (ទ. ៧៩)
BATHTUB អាងទឹក (ទ. ៧៩)
BEAR ខ្លាឃ្មុំ (ទ. ៨៣)
BED គ្រែគេង (ទ. ៧២)
BEDROOM បន្ទប់គេង (ទ. ៧២)
BEE ឃ្មុំ (ទ. ៨៨)
BICYCLE កង់ (ទ. ១៣)
BIG ធំ (ទ. ៣៤)
BIRD សត្វស្លាប (ទ. ៨៨)
BITE ខាំ (ទ. ៨០)
BLOOD លោហិត ឬឈាម (ទ. ៨០)
BOAT កាណូត (ទ. ១៣)
BORED អផ្សុក បុក្ខុទ្រាទ (ទ. ២៦)
BOY ក្មេងប្រុស (ទ. ៦២)
BRAVE ក្លាហាន (ទ. ២៦)
BRIGHT ភ្លឺ (ទ. ៣៤)
BROTHER បង បឬ្អូនប្រុស (ទ. ១៤)
BRUISE ស្នាមជាំ (ទ. ៨០)
BUILD ស្ថាបនា (ទ. ២)
BURN រលាក (ទ. ៨០)
BUS ឡានក្រុង (ទ. ១៣)
BUSDRIVER អ្នកបើកឡានក្រុង(ទ.៦២)
BUTTERFLY មេអំបៅ (ទ. ៨៨)

C
CAR រថយន្តឬឡាន (ទ. ១៣)
CARPENTER ជាងឈើ (ទ. ៦២)
CAT ឆ្មា (ទ. ៨៩)
CATCH ចាប់ (ទ. ២)
CHAIR កៅអី ឬជើងម៉ា (ទ. ៧២)
CHASE រត់ដេញ (ទ. ៣)
CHEF ចុងភៅ (ទ. ៦៣)
CHICKEN មាន់ (ទ. ៨៩)
CHILDREN ក្មេងៗ (ទ. ៦៣)
CLEAN សំអាត, ស្អាត (ទ. ៣, ៣៤)
CLIMB ឡើង (ទ. ៣)
CLOSED ហាងបិទទ្វា (ទ. ៦៣)
CLOWN តុក (ទ. ៦៣)
COLD រងារ ឬត្រជាក់ (ទ. ៣៤)
COOK ចុងភៅ (ទ. ៦)
COW គោ (ទ. ៨៩)
CRAYON ខ្មៅដៃពណ៌ (ទ. ៨៣)
CRY យំ (ទ. ៦)
CURTAIN រាំងនន (ទ. ៧៣)
CUT មុត (ទ. ៨១)

D
DANCE រាំ (ទ. ៦)
DANCER អ្នករាំ (ទ. ៦៤)
DARK យប់ងងឹត (ទ. ៣៥)
DEER ក្ដាន់ (ទ. ៨៥)
DENTIST ពេទ្យធ្មេញ (ទ. ៦៤)
DIFFICULT ពិបាកធ្វើកិច្ចការ (ទ.៣៥)
DIG ជីកដី (ទ. ៧)
DINOSAUR សត្វដីណូស័រ (ទ. ៨៥)
DIRTY ប្រឡាក់ក្រខ្វក់ (ទ. ៣៥)
DIVE លោតមុជទៅទឹក (ទ. ៦)
DOCTOR វេជ្ជបណ្ឌិត (ទ. ៦៦)
DOG ឆ្កែ (ទ. ៩០)
DOLL កូនក្រមុំកាស្ស៊ូ (ទ. ៨៣)
DOOR ទ្វា (ទ. ៧៣)
DOWN ចុះក្រោម (ទ. ៦៨)
DRAW គូររូប (ទ. ៦)
DREAM សុបិន (ទ. ៦)
DRESSER ទូដាក់គ្រឿងសំអាង(ទ.៧៣)
DRINK ផឹក (ទ. ៦)
DRIVE បររថយន្ត (ទ. ៦)
DRY ផ្ដិតស្ងួត (ទ. ៦៨)
DRYER ម៉ាស៊ីនហាលសំលៀកអាវ (ទ.៧៨)
DUCK សត្វទា (ទ. ៨៩)

E
EASY ឆាយស្រួល (ទ. ៣៥)
EAT ញ៉ាំ (ទ. ៧)
ELEPHANT ដំរី (ទ. ៨៩)
EMBARRASSED ខ្មាស់អៀន (ទ. ២៦)
EXCITED រំភើបចិត្ត (ទ. ២៧)

F
FAKE ក្លែងក្លាយ (ទ. ៦៣)
FALL ធ្លាក់ចុះ (ទ. ៧)
FAMILY គ្រួសារ (ទ. ១៣)
FAR ឆ្ងាយ (ទ. ៦៩)
FARMER អ្នកចំការ (ទ. ៦៦)
FAT ធាត់ (ទ. ៣៥)
FATHER ឪពុក (ទ. ១៤)
FEED ឲ្យចំណីអាហារ (ទ. ៧)
FEEL ស្ទាបមើល (ទ. ៨)
FEW ខ្លះ (ទ.៦៩)
FIND រកឃើញ (ទ. ៨)
FIREFIGHTER អ្នកពន្លត់ភ្លើង(ទ.៦៦)
FISH សួរត្រី, ត្រី (ទ.៨, ៩១)
FISHERMAN អ្នកនេសាទ (ទ. ៦៦)
FLOWER ផ្កា (ទ. ៨៧)
FLY ហោះហើរ (ទ. ៩)
FLY-A-KITE បង្ហោះខ្លែង (ទ. ៩)
FOOLISH ភ្លីភ្លើ (ទ. ២៧)
FOX កញ្ជ្រោង (ទ. ៩២)
FRIEND សម្លាញ់ (ទ. ៦៣)
FRIENDLY ចិត្តភាព (ទ. ២៧)
FROG កង្កែប (ទ. ៩២)
FRUSTRATED ម្លេម៉ៅ (ទ. ២៧)
FULL ឆ្អែត (ទ. ៣៥)

G
GAME ល្បែងកីឡាសន្ត (ទ. ៨៦)
GARAGE បន្ទប់ចតរថយន្ត (ទ. ៧៦)
GIRAFFE សត្វឆ្កត វែង (ទ. ៨៩)
GIRL ក្មេងស្រី (ទ. ៦៣)
GIVE ឲ្យ (ទ. ៩)
GRANDFATHER តា (ទ. ១៤)
GRANDMOTHER យាយ (ទ. ១៤)
GRASS ស្មៅ។ (ទ. ៨៧)

H
HAPPY រីករាយ (ទ. ២៧)
HARD ពិបាកចិត្ត (ទ. ៣៥)
HE គាត់ (កេរប្រុស) (ទ.១០២)
HEAVY ធ្ងន់ (ទ. ៣៥)
HELICOPTER ឧទ្ធម្ភាគចក្រ (ទ. ១៣)
HELP ជួយ (ទ. ១០)
HER គាត់ (កេរស្រី) (ទ.១០២)
HIDE លាក់ (ទ. ១០)
HIGH ខ្ពស់ (ទ. ៣៥)

HIM គាត់ (កេរប្រុស) (ទ.១០២)
HIS របស់គាត់ (កេរប្រុស) (ទ.១០២)
HIT វាយទិនដិបល (ទ. ១០)
HORSE សេះ (ទ. ៩៣)
HOT ក្ដៅ (ទ. ៣៣)
HOUSE ផ្ទះ (ទ. ៧៣)
HUNGRY ឃ្លាន (ទ. ៣៩)
HURT ឈឺអារម្មណ៍ (ទ. ២៧)

I
I ខ្ញុំ (ប្រើជាប្រធាន) (ទ.១០២)
ICE SKATE លេងប៉ាតាំង (ទ. ១១)
IN ក្នុង (ទ. ៦០)
IT វា (ទ.១០៣)

J
JEALOUS ច្រណែន (ទ. ២៨)
JUMP លោត (ទ. ១១)

K
KISS ថើប (ទ. ១១)
KITCHEN ផ្ទះបាយ (ទ. ៧៦)
KITE ខ្លែង (ទ. ៨៦)
KNIT ចាក់ (អាវយឺត) (ទ. ១២)

L
LAMP ចង្កៀង (ទ. ៧៦)
LAUGH សើច (ទ. ១២)
LIBRARIAN បណ្ណារក្ស (ទ. ៦៣)
LIGHT ស្រាល (ទ. ៣៦)
LION តោ (ទ. ៩៣)
LIVING ROOM
   បន្ទប់ទទួលភ្ញៀវ (ទ. ៧៦)
LONELY ឯកា (ទ. ២៨)
LOSE បាត់បង់ (ទ. ១២)
LOVE ស្រឡាញ់ (ទ. ១៣)
LOW ទាបក្រោម (ទ. ៣៦)

M
MAD ខឹង (ទ. ២៨)
MAGICIAN អ្នកចេះផ្នែកវិជ្ជា(ទ.៦៣)
MAILCARRIER
   អ្នករត់សំបុត្រ (ទ. ៦៣)
MAKE ផ្សំផ្គុំ (ទ. ១៣)
MAN បុរស (ទ. ៦៣)
MANY ច្រើន (ទ. ៦៩)
ME ខ្ញុំ (ប្រើជាកម្មបទ) (ទ.១០២)
MEAN កាច (ទ. ៣០)
MECHANIC ជាងម៉ាស៊ីន (ទ. ៦៤)
MICROWAVE OVEN
   ម៉ាស៊ីនកំដៅ ឬឡកំដៅ(ទ.៧៦)
MINE របស់ខ្ញុំ(ប្រើជាកម្មបទ)(ទ.១០៣)
MONKEY ស្វា (ទ. ៩៣)
MOTHER ម្ដាយ (ទ. ១៤)
MOTORCYCLE ម៉ូតូ (ទ. ១៣)
MOUSE កណ្ដុរ (ទ. ៩៤)
MY របស់ខ្ញុំ(ប្រើជាគុណនាម)(ទ.១០៣)

N
NEAR ជិត (ទ. ៦៩)
NEIGHBOR អ្នកជិតខាង (ទ. ៦៤)
NERVOUS ភ័យផ្ចាញ់ផ្ចាល (ទ. ៣០)
NICE ស្អាត (ទ. ៣០)
NURSE គិលានុបដ្ឋាយិកា (ទ. ៦៧)

O
OLD ចាស់ (ទ. ៨៣)
OPEN ចំហរ (ទ. ៦៧)
OUR
   របស់យើង(ប្រើជាគុណនាម)(ទ.១០៣)
OURS
   របស់យើង(ប្រើជាកម្មបទ)(ទ.១០៣)
OUT ក្រៅ (ទ. ៦៩)

P
PAINT លាបពណ៌ (ទ. ១៣)
PAINTER ជាងលាបថ្នាំ (ទ. ៦៩)
PARENTS ឪពុកម្ដាយ (ទ. ១១)
PEOPLE ប្រជាជន (ទ. ៦៩)
PET អផ្ដែល (ទ. ១៥)
PICTURE រូបគំនូរ (ទ. ៧៦)
PIG ជ្រូក (ទ. ៩៥)
PILOT អ្នកបើកយន្តហោះ (ទ. ៦៩)
PLANT ដាំ, កូនរុក្ខជាតិ(ទ.១៥, ៨៩)
PLAY ប្រឡែងលេង (ទ. ១៥)
POISON ថ្នាំពុល (ទ. ៨១)
POLICE ប៉ូលិស (ទ. ១០)
PRETTY ស្អាត (ទ. ៦២)
PROUD សរសើរ (ទ. ៣១)
PULL អូស ឬទាញ (ទ. ១៥)
PUPPET តុក្កតា (ទ. ៨៦)
PUSH រុញ (ទ. ១៥)
PUT ដាក់ (ទ. ១៥)

R
RABBIT ទន្សាយ (ទ. ៩៥)
RACCOON សំពោច (ទ. ៩៥)
READ អានសៀវភៅ (ទ. ១៦)
REAL ពិត (ទ. ៦២)
REFRIGERATOR ទូទឹកកក (ទ. ៧៦)
RIDE ជិះ (ទ. ៧៦)
ROCKET កាំជ្រួច (ទ. ១៦)
ROCKINGHORSE សេះឈើ (ទ.៨៦)
ROLL រមៀល (ទ. ១៦)
ROLLERSKATE
   ស្បែកជើងវិល មានកង់ (ទ. ១៧)
ROW អុំទូក ឬចែវទូក (ទ. ១៧)
RUN រត់ (ទ. ១៧)

S
SAD ព្រួយ (ទ. ៣១)
SALESPERSON អ្នកលក់ (ទ. ៧០)
SANDBOX កន្លែងដាក់ដីខ្សាច់-
   សំរាប់ឲ្យក្មេងលេង (ទ. ៨៦)
SCARED ខ្លាច (ទ.៣១)
SCIENTIST អ្នកវិទ្យាសាស្ត្រ (ទ. ៧០)
SEARCH ស្រាវជ្រាវ រក (ទ. ១៧)
SEE មើល (ទ. ១៧)
SEESAW
   ក្ដារ(ជិះលេង) បះចុះឡើង (ទ. ៨៦)
SEW ដេរ (ទ. ១៧)
SHE គាត់ (កេរស្រី) (ទ.១០២)
SHEEP ចៀម (ទ. ៩៥)
SHOCK ឆក់ខ្សែភ្លើង (ទ. ៨២)
SHORT ទាប ឬខ្លី (ទ. ៦៦)
SHOWER ទឹកផ្កាឈូក (ទ. ៧៧)
SHY អៀនខ្មាស់ (ទ. ៣២)
SICK ឈឺ (ទ. ៣២)
SILLY រងើវរងាវ (ទ. ៣២)
SINGER អ្នកច្រៀង (ទ. ៧១)
SINK កន្លែងលាងចាន (ទ. ៧៧)
SISTER បង , បឬ្អូនស្រី (ទ. ១១)
SIT អង្គុយ (ទ. ១៨)
SKATEBOARD ក្ដារស្គីត (ទ. ៨៧)
SKUNK ស្កុង (ទ. ៩៥)
SLED តារទឹកកក (ទ. ៨៧)
SLEEP គេង (ទ. ១៨)
SLIDE អ្រិលចុះ (ទ. ១៨)
SMALL តូច (ទ. ៣៦)
SMELL ហិត (ទ. ២០)
SNAKE ពស់ (ទ. ៩៥)
SNOB រាបួយ (ទ. ៣២)
SOFA កៅអ៊ីក្រណាត់វែង (ទ. ៧៧)

SOFT ទន់ (ទ. ៦៦)
SPIDER ពីងពាង (ទ. ៨៩)
SPIN ចងិល (ទ. ២០)
STAND ឈរ (ទ. ២០)
STING ការទិច (ទ. ៨២)
STOVE ចង្ក្រាន (ទ. ៧៧)
SUBWAY ម៉ែត្រូ (ទ. ១៦)
SURPRISE ភ្ញាក់ផ្អើល (ទ. ៣៣)
SWIM ហែលទឹក (ទ. ២១)
SWING យោលយោង (ទ. ២១)

T
TABLE តុ (ទ. ៧៧)
TAKE យក (ទ. ២១)
TALK កិភាគសារគ្នា (ទ. ២២)
TALL ខ្ពស់ (ទ. ៦៦)
TASTE ភ្លក់ (ទ. ២២)
TEACHER គ្រូ (ទ. ៧១)
THEIR
   របស់ពួកគេ (ប្រើជាគុណនាម) (ទ.១០៣)
THEIRS
   របស់ពួកគេ (ប្រើជាកម្មបទ) (ទ.១០៣)
THEM ពួកគេ(ប្រើជាកម្មបទ)(ទ.១០៣)
THEY ពួកគេ(ប្រើជាប្រធាន)(ទ.១០៣)
THIEF ចោរ (ទ. ៧១)
THIN ស្គម (ទ. ៣៦)
THIRSTY ស្រេកទឹក (ទ. ៣៣)
THROW ចោល (ទ. ២២)
TIGER ខ្លា (ទ. ៩៥)
TIP TOE ដើរចុងជើង (ទ. ២៣)
TIRED អស់កម្លាំង (ទ. ៣៣)
TOILET បង្គន់ (ទ. ៧៧)
TOYS ប្រដាប់ប្រដាលេង (ទ. ៨៣)
TRADE ប្ដូរគ្នា (ទ. ២៣)
TRAIN រថភ្លើង (ទ. ៧០)
TRANSPORTATION
   យានជំនិះ (ទ. ៧០)
TRASH CAN ធុងសំរាម (ទ. ៧៩)
TREE ដើមឈើ (ទ. ៨៩)
TRUCK ឡានដឹកទំនិញ (ទ. ៧០)
TURKEY មាន់បារាំង (ទ. ៨៩)
TURTLE អណ្ដើក (ទ. ៨៩)

U
UGLY អាក្រក់មើល (ទ. ៦៣)
UNCLE ពូ ឬពុកមា (ទ. ១១)
UP នៅលើ (ទ. ៦៩)
US យើង (ប្រើជាកម្មបទ) (ទ.១០៣)

V
VETERINARIAN ពេទ្យសត្វ (ទ. ៧២)

W
WAITRESS ស្រ្តីបរិវេណ (ទ. ៧២)
WALK ដើរ (ទ. ២៣)
WASH លាង (ទ. ២៦)
WASHING MACHINE
   ម៉ាស៊ីនបោក ខោអាវ (ទ. ៧៨)
WATCH មើល (ទ. ២៦)
WE យើង (ប្រើជាប្រធាន) (ទ.១០៣)
WELL ស្រួលខ្លួន (ទ. ៦៦)
WET ទទឹក (ទ. ៦៩)
WINDOW បង្អួច (ទ. ៧៨)
WOLF ឆ្កែចចក (ទ. ៨៩)
WOMAN ស្ត្រី (ទ. ១០២)
WRITE សរសេរអក្សរ (ទ. ២៦)

Y
YOUNG វ័យក្មេង (ទ. ៦៣)
YOU អ្នក (ប្រើជាប្រធាន) (ទ.១០៣)
YOU ALL អ្នកទាំងអស់គ្នា (ទ.១០៣)
YOUR របស់អ្នក(ប្រើជាគុណនាម)(ទ.១០៣)
YOURS របស់អ្នក(ប្រើជាកម្មបទ)(ទ.១០៣)

A
ACT UA QHIA p. 2
ACTOR TUS NEEG UA QHIA p. 50
ADULT NEEG LAUS p. 50
AIRPLANE DAV HLAU p. 67
ALLIGATOR TUS KHEB p. 87
ANIMALS COV TSIAJ p. 87
ARTIST COV NEEG KOS DUAB p. 50
AUNT PHAUJ p. 64

B
BABY MOS AB (LIAB) p. 51
BABYSITTER NEEG ZOV ME NYUAM p. 51
BALL LUB POB p. 83
BARBER NEEG TXIAV PLAUB HAU p. 51
BASEMENT QAB TSEV p. 71
BATHROOM CHAV DEJ p. 71
BATHTUB DAB DEJ p. 71
BEAR DAIS p. 87
BED TXAJ PW p. 72
BEDROOM CHAV TSEV PW p. 72
BEE MUV p. 88
BICYCLE TSHEB KAUJ VAB p. 67
BIG LOJ p. 34
BIRD NOOG p. 88
BITE TOM p. 80
BLOOD NTSHAV p. 80
BOAT NKOJ p. 67
BORED DHUAV p. 26
BOY LEEJ TUB p. 52
BRAVE SIAB TAWV p. 26
BRIGHT CI p. 34
BROTHER KWV TIJ LEEJ NUS p. 64
BRUISE DOOG p. 80
BUILD TEEB p. 2
BURN KUB NYHIAB p. 81
BUS TSHEB THAUJ NEEG p. 68
BUSDRIVER NEEG TSAV TSHEB p. 52
BUTTERFLY NPAUJ NPAIM p. 88

C
CAR TSHEB p. 68
CARPENTER NEEG UA TSEV p. 52
CAT MIV p. 89
CATCH TXHOM, NTES p. 2
CHAIR ROOJZAUM p. 72
CHASE CAUM QAB p. 3
CHEF NEEG SAIB XYUAS ZAUB MOV p. 53
CHICKEN QAIB p. 89
CHILDREN COV ME NYUAM p. 53
CLEAN NTXHUA p. 34
CLIMB NCE p. 3
CLOSED KAW LAWM p. 43
CLOWN YAWG ZAB p. 53
COLD NO p. 36
COOK UA MOV NOJ p. 36
COW NYUJ p. 89
CRAYON CWJ MEM QHUAV ZAS p. 83
CRY QUAJ p. 4
CURTAIN NTAUB THAIV QHOV RAIS p. 73
CUT HLAIS p. 81

D
DANCE NCHOV CEV p. 4
DANCER NEEG NCHOV CEV p. 54
DARK TSAUS NTUJ p. 35
DEER MOS LWJ p. 90

DENTIST KWV KHO HNIAV p. 54
DIFFICULT NYUAB p. 36
DIG KHAWB p. 5
DINOSAUR TUS DINOSAUR p. 90
DIRTY LO AV p. 35
DIVE DIA DEJ p. 5
DOCTOR KWS KHO MOB p. 54
DOG DEV p. 90
DOLL NEEG ROJ HNAB p. 83
DOOR QHOV ROOJ p. 73
DOWN QIS p. 47
DRAW KOS DUAB p. 5
DREAM NPAUS UAV p. 6
DRESSER TUB RAU KHOOM p. 73
DRINK HAUS p. 6
DRIVE TSAV TSHEB p. 6
DRY TSHUAB PLAUB HAU p. 47
DRYER LUB ZIAB KHAUB NCAWS p. 74
DUCK OS p. 91

E
EASY YOOJ YIM p. 37
EAT NOJ p. 7
ELEPHANT NTXHW p. 91
EMBARRASSED NYUAB SLAB p. 26
EXCITED ZOO SLAB HEEV p. 27

F
FAKE CUAV p. 43
FALL POOB p. 7
FAMILY TSEV NEEG p. 63
FAR DEB p. 41
FARMER NEEG UA TEB p. 55
FAT ROG p. 36
FATHER LEEJ TXIV p. 64
FEED PUB NOJ p. 7
FEEL HNOV p. 8
FEW OB PEB TUG p. 41
FIND NRHIAV p. 8
FIREFIGHTER NEEG TUA HLUAV TAWS p. 55
FISH NTSES p. 8, 91
FISHERMAN NEEG NUV (CUAB) NTSES p. 55
FLOWER PAJ p. 98
FLY YA p. 9
FLY-A-KITE TSO-KITE YA p. 9
FOOLISH NCAWB p. 27
FOX HMA p. 92
FRIEND PHOOJ YWG p. 56
FRIENDLY ZOO PHOOJ YWG p. 27
FROG QAV p. 92
FRUSTRATED YOOB p. 28
FULL TSAU PLAB p. 38

G
GAME KHOOM UA SI p. 84
GARAGE CHAW RAU TSHEB p. 74
GIRAFFE TUS GIRAFFE p. 92
GIRL LEEJ NTXHAIS p. 56
GIVE MUAB PUB p. 9
GRANDFATHER YAWG p. 65
GRANDMOTHER POG p. 65
GRASS NYOM p. 98

H
HAPPY ZOO SIAB p. 28
HARD NYUAB p. 45
HE NWS p. 102
HEAVY NYHAV p. 38
HELICOPTER NYOB HOOM TSHUAB p. 68
HELP PAB p. 10
HER NWS p. 102
HERS NWS LI p. 102
HIDE TSIV NKAUM p. 10

HIGH SIAB p. 38
HIM NWS p. 102
HIS NWS LI p. 102
HIT NTAUS p. 10
HORSE NEES p. 93
HOT TSHAV KUB p. 37
HOUSE LUB TSEV p. 74
HUNGRY TSHAIB PLAB p. 39
HURT CHIM SIAB p. 28

I
I KUV p. 102
ICE SKATE CAIJ KHAU MUS SAUM COV DEJ KHOV p. 11
IN NYOB HAUV p. 40
IT NWS p. 103

J
JEALOUS MUAJ KHIB p. 29
JUMP DHIA p. 11

K
KISS SIB NHIA p. 11
KITCHEN CHAV TSEV UA MOV NOJ p. 75
KITE TUS KITE p. 84
KNIT QHAIB p. 12

L
LAMP LUB TEEB p. 75
LAUGH LUAG p. 12
LIBRARIAN NEEG XYUAS NTAUB NTAWV p. 56
LIGHT SIB p. 39
LION TSOV NTXHUAV p. 93
LIVING ROOM CHAV TSEV NYOB p. 75
LONELY NYOB IB LEEG p. 29
LOSE POOB p. 12
LOVE HLUB p. 13
LOW QIS p. 39

M
MAD CHIM SIAB p. 29
MAGICIAN NEEG UA YEEB YAM p. 57
MAILCARRIER NEEG XA NTAWV p. 57
MAKE UA p. 13
MAN TXIV NEEJ p. 57
MANY COOB, NTAU p. 40
ME KUV p. 102
MEAN NEEG SIAB PHEM p. 30
MECHANIC NEEG KHO TSHEB p. 58
MICROWAVE OVEN TSHUAB CI NQAIJ p. 76
MINE KUV LI p. 103
MONKEY LIAB p. 93
MOTHER LEEJ NIAM p. 65
MOTORCYCLE LUB LAUV CAV p. 69
MOUSE NAS TSUAG p. 94
MY KUV p. 103

N
NEAR ZE p. 40
NEIGHBOR NEEG ZOG p. 58
NERVOUS POOB SIAB p. 30
NICE UA ZOO p. 30
NURSE NEEG SAIB MOB p. 58

O
OLD LAUS p. 47
OPEN QHIB p. 42
OUR PEB p. 103
OURS PEB LI p. 103
OUT KHIAV MUS p. 41

P
PAINT PLEEV XIM p. 13
PAINTER TUS NEEG PLEEV XIM p. 59

PARENTS LEEJ NIAM THIAB LEEJ TXIV p. 66

PEOPLE TIB NEEG p. 59
PET TSIAJ p. 14
PICTURE DAIM DUAB p. 76
PIG NPUA p. 94
PILOT NEEG TSAV DAV HLAU p. 59
PLANT NROOJ p. 14, 99
PLAY UA SI p. 14
POISON T SHUAJ LOM p. 81
POLICE TUB CEEV XWM p. 60
PRETTY ZOO NKAUJ p. 42
PROUD ZOO SIAB HLO p. 31
PULL CAB p. 15
PUPPET MAJ ZEEJ p. 84
PUSH THAWB p. 15
PUT TXAWB p. 15

R
RABBIT LUAV p. 94
RACCOON TUS RACCOON p. 95
READ NYEEM NTAWV p. 16
REAL TIAG p. 42
REFRIGERATOR LUB TXEE TXIAS p. 76
RIDE CAIJ p. 16
ROCKET LUB CUAB LUAJ p. 69
ROCKINGHORSE TUS NEES NTOO p. 85
ROLL TSO CEV NTOG p. 16
ROLLERSKATE CAIJ KHAU LOG p. 17
ROW NQUAM NKOJ p. 17
RUN KHIAV p. 17

S
SAD MLUAS p. 31
SALESPERSON NEEG MUAG KHOOM p. 60
SANDBOX THAWV SUAB ZEB p. 85
SCARED NTSHAI p. 31
SCIENTIST NEEG SCIENTIST p. 60
SEARCH NRHIAV p. 18
SEE POM p. 18
SEESAW UA DEV TUAV COS p. 85
SEW XAWS p. 18
SHE NWS p. 102
SHEEP YAJ p. 95
SHOCK HLUAV TAWS XOB NQUS p. 82
SHORT QIG TAUB p. 44
SHOWER TUS CAIV DEJ NTXUAV CEV p. 77
SHY TXAJ MUAG p. 32
SICK MOB p. 44
SILLY UA ZOO LI ME NYUAM YAUS p. 32
SINGER NEEG HU NKAUJ p. 61
SINK DAB NTXUAV MUAG p. 77
SISTER TUS MUAM TUS NIAM LAUS p. 66
SIT ZAUM p. 19
SKATEBOARD DAIM TXIAG KHAU LOG p. 86
SKUNK NTXIM TSUAG p. 95
SLED CAIJ TXIAG p. 86
SLEEP PW p. 19
SLIDE UA LUAV LUAM p. 19
SMALL ME p. 35
SMELL HNIAV p. 20
SNAKE NAB p. 96
SNOB UA ZOO LITUS NEEG NTSE p. 32
SOFA ROOJ SOFA p. 77
SOFT ZOOJ p. 44
SPIDER KAB LAUG SAB p. 96
SPIN KIV p. 20
STAND SAWV p. 20

STING PLEV p. 82
STOVE QHOV CUB p. 78
SUBWAY KEV QHOV AV p. 69
SURPRISE RAS DHEEV p. 33
SWIM UA LUAM DEJ p. 21
SWING UA VIAV VIAS p. 21

T
TABLE ROOJ LOJ p. 78
TAKE NQA p. 21
TALK SIB THAM p. 22
TALL SIAB p. 45
TASTE SAJ p. 22
TEACHER KWS QHIA NTAWV p. 61
THEIR LAWV p. 104
THEIRS LAWV LI p. 104
THEM LAWV p. 104
THEY LAWV p. 104
THIEF TUB SAB p. 61
THIN CEV NYIAS, los yog CEV YUAG p. 37
THIRSTY NQHIS DEJ p. 33
THROW POV, TXAWB p. 22
TIGER TSOV p. 96
TIP TOE SIV NTSIS NTIV TAWS MUS KEV p. 23
TIRED NKEES p. 33
TOILET DAB DEJ TSO QUAV p. 78
TOYS COV KHOOM UA SI p. 86
TRADE SIB PAUV p. 23
TRAIN TSHEB LAUV FAIS p. 70
TRANSPORTATION KEV CAIJ TSHEB MUS LOS SIB CUAG p. 70
TRASH THOOB NTIM KHOOM POV TSEG p. 79
TREE TSOB NTOO p. 99
TRUCK TSHEB THAUJ KHOOM p. 70
TURKEY QAIB NCOV TXWV p. 97
TURTLE VAUB KIB p. 97

U
UGLY QIAS NEEG p. 43
UNCLE TXIV TXAWM, TXIV HLOB p. 66
UP NCE SIAB p. 46
US PEB p. 104

V
VETERINARIAN KWS KHO TSIAJ p. 62

W
WAITRESS TUS POJ NIAM RAU ZAUB MOV p. 62
WALK MUS KEV p. 23
WASH TXUAV p. 24
WASHING MACHINE LUB TSHUAB TXHUA KHAUB NCAWS p. 79
WATCH SAIB, NTSIA p. 24
WE PEB p. 104
WELL ZOO p. 45
WET NTUB p. 46
WINDOW QHOV RAIS p. 79
WOLF HMA p. 97
WOMAN POJ NIAM p. 62
WRITE SAU NTAWV p. 24

Y
YOUNG HLUAS p. 46
YOU KOJ p. 105
YOU ALL NEJ TAS NRHO p.105
YOUR KOJ LI p. 105
YOURS NEJ LI p. 105

ຈັດລຽງຕາມລຳດັບໂຕອັກສອນ

A / ເອ
ACT p.2 — ສະແດງ ໜ.2
ACTOR p.50 — ຜູ້ສະແດງ ໜ.50
ADULT p.50 — ຜູ້ໃຫຍ່ ໜ.50
AIRPLANE p.67 — ເຮືອບິນ ໜ.67
ALLIGATOR p.87 — ແຂ້ ໜ.87
ANIMALS p.87 — ພວກສັດ ໜ.87
ARTIST p.50 — ນັກແຕ້ມ ໜ.50
AUNT p.64 — ປ້າ ໜ.64

B / ບີ
BABY p.51 — ເດັກນ້ອຍ ໜ.51
BABYSITTER p.51 — ຄົນລ້ຽງເດັກ ໜ.51
BALL p.83 — ໝາກບານ ໜ.83
BARBER p.51 — ຊ່າງຕັດຜົມ ໜ.51
BASEMENT p.71 — ຫ້ອງໃຕ້ດິນ ໜ.71
BATHROOM p.71 — ຫ້ອງນ້ຳ ໜ.71
BATHTUB p.71 — ອ່າງອາບນ້ຳ ໜ.71
BEAR p.87 — ໝີ ໜ.87
BED p.72 — ຕຽງນອນ ໜ.72
BEDROOM p.72 — ຫ້ອງນອນ ໜ.72
BEE p.88 — ແມງເຜິ້ງ ໜ.88
BICYCLE p.67 — ລົດຖີບ ໜ.67
BIG p.34 — ໃຫຍ່ ໜ.34
BIRD p.88 — ນົກ ໜ.88
BITE p.80 — ກັດ ໜ.80
BLOOD p.80 — ເລືອດ ໜ.80
BOAT p.67 — ເຮືອ ໜ.67
BORED p.26 — ເບື່ອຣະອາ ໜ.26
BOY p.52 — ເດັກຜູ້ຊາຍ ໜ.52
BRAVE p.26 — ກ້າຫານ ໜ.26
BRIGHT p.34 — ໃສແຈ້ງ ໜ.34
BROTHER p.64 — ອ້າຍ/ນ້ອງຊາຍ ໜ.64
BRUISE p.80 — ຮອຍຊ້ຳ ໜ.80
BUILD p.2 — ກໍ່ສ້າງ ໜ.2
BURN p.81 — ໄໝ້ ໜ.81
BUS p.68 — ລົດເມ ໜ.68
BUSDRIVER p.52 — ຄົນຂັບລົດເມ ໜ.52
BUTTERFLY p.88 — ແມງກະເບື້ອ ໜ.88

C / ຊີ
CAR p.68 — ລົດ ໜ.68
CARPENTER p.52 — ຊ່າງໄມ້ ໜ.52
CAT p.89 — ແມວ ໜ.89
CATCH p.2 — ຈັບໄດ້ ໜ.2
CHAIR p.72 — ຕັ່ງ ໜ.72
CHASE p.3 — ໄລ່ຕາມ ໜ.3
CHEF p.53 — ຫົວໜ້າພໍ່ຄົວ ໜ.53
CHICKEN p.89 — ໄກ່ ໜ.89
CHILDREN p.53 — ເດັກນ້ອຍຫລາຍຄົນ ໜ.53
CLEAN p.3,34 — ທຳຄວາມສະອາດ ໜ.3,34
CLIMB p.3 — ປີນຂຶ້ນ ໜ.3
CLOSED p.43 — ອັກແລ້ວ ໜ.43
CLOWN p.53 — ຕົວຕະຫລົກ ໜ.53
COLD p.36 — ໜາວ ໜ.36
COOK p.4 — ຄົນຄົວກິນ ໜ.4
COW p.89 — ງົວ ໜ.89
CRAYON p.83 — ສີທຽນ ໜ.83
CRY p.4 — ຮ້ອງໄຫ້ ໜ.4
CURTAIN p.73 — ຜ້າກັ້ງ ໜ.73
CUT p.81 — ຕັດ ໜ.81

D / ດີ
DANCE p.4 — ເຕັ້ນລຳ ໜ.4
DANCER p.54 — ຜູ້ເຕັ້ນລຳ ໜ.54
DARK p.35 — ມືດ ໜ.35
DEER p.90 — ກວາງ ໜ.90
DENTIST p.54 — ໝໍປົວແຂ້ວ ໜ.54
DIFFICULT p.36 — ຍຸ້ງຍາກ ໜ.36
DIG p.5 — ຂຸດ ໜ.5
DINOSAUR p.90 — ໄດໂນເຊົາ ໜ.90
DIRTY p.35 — ເປື້ອນ ໜ.35
DIVE p.5 — ໂດດລົງ ໜ.5
DOCTOR p.54 — ທ່ານໝໍ ໜ.54
DOG p.90 — ໝາ ໜ.90
DOLL p.83 — ຕຸກກະຕາ ໜ.83
DOOR p.73 — ປະຕູ ໜ.73
DOWN p.47 — ລົງລຸ່ມ ໜ.47
DRAW p.5 — ແຕ້ມຮູບ ໜ.5
DREAM p.6 — ຝັນ ໜ.6
DRESSER p.73 — ໂຕະແຕ່ງໂຕ ໜ.73
DRINK p.6 — ກິນນ້ຳ ໜ.6
DRIVE p.6 — ຂັບລົດ ໜ.6
DRY p.47 — ຫາກ/ແຫ້ງ ໜ.47
DRYER p.74 — ເຄື່ອງອົບຫາກ ໜ.74
DUCK p.91 — ເປັດ ໜ.91

E / ອີ
EASY p.37 — ງ່າຍ ໜ.37
EAT p.7 — ກິນ ໜ.7
ELEPHANT p.91 — ຊ້າງ ໜ.91
EMBARRASSED p.26 — ຫຍຸ້ງໃຈອັບອາຍ ໜ.26
EXCITED p.27 — ຕື່ນເຕັ້ນ ໜ.27

F / ແອັຟ
FAKE p.43 — ຂອງປອມ ໜ.43
FALL p.7 — ຕົກ ໜ.7
FAMILY p.63 — ຄອບຄົວ ໜ.63
FAR p.41 — ທ່າງໄກ ໜ.41
FARMER p.55 — ຊາວນາ ໜ.55
FAT p.36 — ຕຸ້ຍ ໜ.36
FATHER p.64 — ພໍ່ ໜ.64
FEED p.7 — ປ້ອນເຂົ້າ ໜ.7
FEEL p.8 — ຈັບບຼ່ງຄວາມຮູ້ສຶກ ໜ.8
FEW p.41 — ສອງສາມບຼ່ງ ໜ.41
FIND p.8 — ຟົບເຫັນ ໜ.8
FIREFIGHTER p.55 — ນັກດັບເພີງ ໜ.55
FISH p.8, 91 — ປາ ໜ.8,91
FISHERMAN p.55 — ຄົນຫາປາ ໜ.55
FLOWER p.98 — ດອກໄມ້ ໜ.98
FLY p.9 — ບິນ ໜ.9
FLY-A-KITE p.9 — ປ່ອຍວ່າວ ໜ.9
FOOLISH p.27 — ບ້າໆບໍໆ ໜ.27
FOX p.92 — ໝາຈອກ ໜ.92
FRIEND p.56 — ໝູ່ຄູ່ ໜ.56
FRIENDLY p.27 — ຄຸ້ນເຄີຍ ໜ.27
FROG p.92 — ກົບ ໜ.92
FRUSTRATED p.28 — ຍຸ້ມທໍ້ວ້າ ໜ.28
FULL p.38 — ອິ່ມ/ເຕັມ ໜ.38

G / ຈີ
GAME p.84 — ການຫລິ້ນ ໜ.84
GARAGE p.74 — ລອງເກັບລົດ ໜ.74
GIRAFFE p.92 — ໂຕຄໍຍາວຄໍຍາວ ໜ.92
GIRL p.56 — ເດັກຜູ້ຍິງ ໜ.56
GIVE p.9 — ເອົາໃຫ້ ໜ.9
GRANDFATHER p.65 — ພໍ່ເຖົ້າ ໜ.65
GRANDMOTHER p.65 — ແມ່ເຖົ້າ ໜ.65
GRASS p.98 — ຫຍ້າ/ຕົ້ນຫຍ້າ ໜ.98

H / ເອັຊ
HAPPY p.28 — ເບີກບານໃຈ ໜ.28
HARD p.45 — ຍາກ ໜ.45
HE p.102 — ເຂົາຜູ້ຊາຍ ໜ.102
HEAVY p.38 — ໜັກ ໜ.38
HELICOPTER p.68 — ຍົນຂວດຂອດ ໜ.68
HELP p.10 — ຊ່ອຍ ໜ.10
HER p.102 — ຂອງເຂົາຜູ້ຍິງ ໜ.102
HERS p.102 — ຂອງພວກເຂົາຜູ້ຍິງ ໜ.102
HIDE p.10 — ລີ້ ໜ.10
HIGH p.38 — ສູງ ໜ.38
HIM p.102 — ເຂົາຜູ້ຊາຍ ໜ.102
HIS p.102 — ຂອງເຂົາຜູ້ຊາຍ ໜ.102
HIT p.10 — ຕີໃສ່/ຕ່ອຍ ໜ.10
HORSE p.93 — ມ້າ ໜ.93
HOT p.37 — ຮ້ອນ ໜ.37
HOUSE p.74 — ເຮືອນ ໜ.74
HUNGRY p.39 — ຫິວເຂົ້າ ໜ.39
HURT p.28 — ທຳຄວາມຮູ້ສຶກ ໜ.28

I / ໄອ
I p.102 — ຂ້ອຍ ໜ.102
ICE SKATE p.11 — ແລ່ນສະເກັດນ້ຳກ້ອນ ໜ.11
IN p.40 — ຢູ່ໃນ ໜ.40
IT p.103 — ມັນ/ສິ່ງຂອງ ໜ.103

J / ເຈ
JEALOUS p.29 — ອິດສາ ໜ.29
JUMP p.11 — ໂດດ ໜ.11

K / ເຄ
KISS p.11 — ຈູບ ໜ.11
KITCHEN p.75 — ເຮືອນຄົວ ໜ.75
KITE p.84 — ວ່າວ ໜ.84
KNIT p.12 — ຖັກແສ່ວດ້ວຍກ່ານ ໜ.12

L / ແອລ
LAMP p.75 — ໂຄມໄຟ ໜ.75
LAUGH p.12 — ຫົວ ໜ.12
LIBRARIAN p.56 — ຄຼູຫ້ອງສະໝຸດ ໜ.56
LIGHT p.39 — ຂີ້ວ່າ ໜ.39
LION p.93 — ສິງ ໜ.93
LIVING ROOM p.75 — ຫ້ອງຮັບແຂກ ໜ.75

M
LONELY p.29 — ເຫງົາເປົ່າ ໜ.29
LOSE p.12 — ເສຍ/ເສັຽ ໜ.12
LOVE p.13 — ຮັກ ໜ.13
LOW p.39 — ຕ່ຳ ໜ.39

M / ເອັມ
MAD p.29 — ຮ້າຍ ໜ.29
MAGICIAN p.57 — ນັກຫລິ້ນກົນ ໜ.57
MAILCARRIER p.57 — ຄົນສົ່ງນ້ວສິ ໜ.57
MAKE p.13 — ເຮັດ/ສ້າງ ໜ.13
MAN p.57 — ຜູ້ຊາຍ ໜ.57
MANY p.40 — ຫລາຍ ໜ.40
ME p.102 — ຂອຍ/ກັບຂອຍ ໜ.102
MEAN p.30 — ໃຈຮ້າຍ/ຈຸ່ງ ໜ.30
MECHANIC p.58 — ຊ່າງແປງລົດ ໜ.58
MICROWAVE OVEN p.76 — ເຕົາອົບອາຫານ ໜ.76
MINE p.103 — ຂອງຂອຍ ໜ.103
MONKEY p.93 — ລີງ ໜ.93
MOTHER p.65 — ແມ່ ໜ.65
MOTORCYCLE p.69 — ລົດຈັກ ໜ.69
MOUSE p.94 — ໜູ ໜ.94
MY p.103 — ຂອງຂອຍ ໜ.103

N / ແອັນ
NEAR p.40 — ໃກ້ ໜ.40
NEIGHBOR p.58 — ມ້ານໃກ້ເຮືອນ ໜ.58
NERVOUS p.30 — ຢ້ານ/ບໍ່ກ້າທຳ ໜ.30
NICE p.30 — ສວຍງາມ ໜ.30
NURSE p.58 — ແພດ ໜ.58

O / ໂອ
OLD p.47 — ເຖົ້າແກ່ ໜ.47
OPEN p.42 — ເປີດ/ໄຂ ໜ.42
OUR p.103 — ຂອງພວກເຮົາ ໜ.103
OURS p.103 — ຂອງພວກເຮົາ ໜ.103
OUT p.41 — ທາງນອກ ໜ.41

P / ພີ
PAINT p.13 — ທາສີ ໜ.13
PAINTER p.59 — ຊ່າງທາສີ ໜ.59
PARENTS p.66 — ພໍ່ແມ່ ໜ.66
PEOPLE p.59 — ປະຊາຊົນ ໜ.59
PET p.14 — ສັດລ້ຽງປູ່ຮ້ອມ ໜ.14
PICTURE p.76 — ຮູບ ໜ.76
PIG p.94 — ໝູ ໜ.94
PILOT p.59 — ນັກຂັບຍົນ ໜ.59
PLANT p.14, 99 — ຕົ້ນໄມ້/ປູກ ໜ.14,99
PLAY p.14 — ຫລິ້ນ ໜ.14
POISON p.81 — ຢາພິດ ໜ.81
POLICE p.60 — ຕຳຫລວດ ໜ.60
PRETTY p.42 — ສວຍງາມ ໜ.42
PROUD p.31 — ພາກພູມໃຈ ໜ.31
PULL p.15 — ດຶງມາ ໜ.15
PUPPET p.84 — ຮູບຫຸ່ນ ໜ.84
PUSH p.15 — ຊຸກໄປ ໜ.15
PUT p.15 — ເອົາໃສ່ ໜ.15

R / ອາຣ໌
RABBIT p.94 — ກະຕ່າຍ ໜ.94
RACCOON p.95 — ໝາໝ້ນ ໜ.95
READ p.16 — ອ່ານ ໜ.16
REAL p.42 — ຂອງແທ້ ໜ.42
REFRIGERATOR p.76 — ຕູ້ເຢັນ ໜ.76
RIDE p.16 — ຂີ່ ໜ.16
ROCKET p.69 — ຈະຫລວດ ໜ.69
ROCKINGHORSE p.85 — ມ້າໂຍກເຫລັ້ນຂອງເດັກ ໜ.85
ROLL p.16 — ກິ້ງ ໜ.16
ROLLERSKATE p.17 — ແລ່ນສະເກັດ ໜ.17
ROW p.17 — ພາຍເຮືອ ໜ.17
RUN p.17 — ແລ່ນ ໜ.17

S / ແອັສ
SAD p.31 — ເສົ້າໃຈ ໜ.31
SALESPERSON p.60 — ຄົນຂາຍເຄື່ອງ ໜ.60
SANDBOX p.85 — ອ່າງຕັ່ມຊາຍ ໜ.85
SCARED p.31 — ຕົ່ມຕົກໃຈ ໜ.31
SCIENTIST p.60 — ນັກວິທະຍາສາດ ໜ.60
SEARCH p.18 — ຊອກຫາ ໜ.18
SEE p.18 — ເຫັນ ໜ.18
SEESAW p.85 — ກະດານໂຍກຂຶ້ນລົງ ໜ.85
SEW p.18 — ຫຍິບແສ່ວ ໜ.18
SHE p.102 — ເຂົາຜູ້ຍິງ ໜ.102
SHEEP p.95 — ໂຕແກະ ໜ.95
SHOCK p.82 — ໄຟຊ໊ອກ ໜ.82
SHORT p.44 — ສັ້ນ ໜ.44
SHOWER p.77 — ບົວອາບນ້ຳ ໜ.77

SH...
LONELY p.29 — ເຫງົາ ໜ.29
SHY p.32 — ອ້າຍ ໜ.32
SICK p.44 — ເຈັບໄຂ້ ໜ.44
SILLY p.32 — ບ້າໆບໍໆ ໜ.32
SINGER p.61 — ນັກຮ້ອງ ໜ.61
SINK p.77 — ອ່າງລ້າງໜ້າ ໜ.77
SISTER p.66 — ເອື້ອຍ/ນ້ອງຜູ້ຍິງ ໜ.66
SIT p.19 — ນັ່ງ ໜ.19
SKATEBOARD p.86 — ແປ້ນສະເກັດ ໜ.86
SKUNK p.95 — ໂຕະກຸ້ງ ໜ.95
SLED p.86 — ແປ້ນບ່ຽງຫິມະກ້ອນ ໜ.86
SLEEP p.19 — ນອນ ໜ.19
SLIDE p.19 — ຫລົນຕະລຸດໂຄງ ໜ.19
SMALL p.35 — ນ້ອຍ ໜ.35
SMELL p.20 — ດົມກິນ ໜ.20
SNAKE p.96 — ງູ ໜ.96
SNOB p.32 — ຍຸກຈອງ/ວາງໂຕສູງ ໜ.32
SOFA p.77 — ຕັ່ງນອນໂຊຟາ ໜ.77
SOFT p.44 — ອ່ອນນຸ່ມ ໜ.44
SPIDER p.96 — ຕົວແມງມຸມ ໜ.96
SPIN p.20 — ປັ່ນ ໜ.20
STAND p.20 — ຢືນ ໜ.20
STING p.82 — ຕອດ ໜ.82
STOVE p.78 — ເຕົາໄຟ ໜ.78
SUBWAY p.69 — ລົດໄຟຟ້າໃຕ້ດິນ ໜ.69
SURPRISE p.33 — ແປກໃຈປ່າງ ໜ.33
SWIM p.21 — ລອຍນ້ຳ ໜ.21
SWING p.21 — ໂຍ່ອຍາ ໜ.21

T / ທີ
TABLE p.78 — ໂຕະ ໜ.78
TAKE p.21 — ຈັບເອົາ ໜ.21
TALK p.22 — ປາກເວົ້າ ໜ.22
TALL p.45 — ສູງ ໜ.45
TASTE p.22 — ຊີມຣົສ ໜ.22
TEACHER p.61 — ນາຍຄຼູ ໜ.61
THEIR p.104 — ຂອງພວກເຂົາເຈົ້າ ໜ.104
THEIRS p.104 — ຂອງພວກເຂົາເຈົ້າ ໜ.104
THEM p.104 — ສຳຫລັບພວກເຂົາເຈົ້າ ໜ.104
THEY p.104 — ພວກເຮົາ ໜ.104
THIEF p.61 — ຄົນຂໂມຍ ໜ.61
THIN p.37 — ຈ່ອຍ ໜ.37
THIRSTY p.33 — ຫິວນ້ຳ ໜ.33
THROW p.22 — ຂວ້າງ/ແປນໄປ ໜ.22
TIGER p.96 — ເສືອ ໜ.96
TIP TOE p.23 — ຍ່າງຢ່ອງໄປຕາມປາຍຕີນ ໜ.23
TIRED p.33 — ອ່ອນເພຍ ໜ.33
TOILET p.78 — ຫ້ອງນ້ຳ ໜ.78
TOYS p.86 — ຂອງຫລິ້ນ ໜ.86
TRADE p.23 — ແລກປ່ຽນ ໜ.23
TRAIN p.70 — ລົດໄຟ ໜ.70
TRANSPORTATION p.70 — ພາຫະນະຂົນສົ່ງ ໜ.70
TRASH CAN p.79 — ກ້ອງໃສ່ຂີ້ເຫຍື້ອ ໜ.79
TREE p.99 — ຕົ້ນໄມ້ ໜ.99
TRUCK p.70 — ລົດກຼະ ໜ.70
TURKEY p.97 — ໄກ່ງວງ ໜ.97
TURTLE p.97 — ເຕົ່າ ໜ.97

U / ຢູ
UGLY p.43 — ຂີ້ລາຍ ໜ.43
UNCLE p.66 — ລຸງ ໜ.66
UP p.46 — ຂຶ້ນ ໜ.46
US p.104 — ພວກຂອຍ ໜ.104

V / ວີ
VETERINARIAN p.62 — ທ່ານໝໍປົວສັດ ໜ.62

W / ດັບເບິ້ນຢູ
WAITRESS p.62 — ຄົນເສີບເຄື່ອງ ໜ.62
WALK p.23 — ຍ່າງ ໜ.23
WASH p.24 — ລ້າງ ໜ.24
WASHING MACHINE p.79 — ຈັກຊັກຜ້າ ໜ.79
WATCH p.24 — ເບິ່ງ ໜ.24
WE p.104 — ພວກເຮົາ ໜ.104
WELL p.45 — ດີ ໜ.45
WET p.46 — ປຽກ ໜ.46
WINDOW p.70 — ປ່ອງຢ້ຽມ ໜ.70
WOLF p.97 — ໝາປ່າ ໜ.97
WOMAN p.62 — ຜູ້ຍິງ ໜ.62
WRITE p.24 — ຂຽນ ໜ.24

Y / ວາຍ
YOUNG p.46 — ໜຸ່ມ ໜ.46
YOU p.105 — ເຈົ້າ/ທ່ານ ໜ.105
YOU ALL p.105 — ເຈົ້າ/ທ່ານທຸກຄົນ ໜ.105
YOUR p.105 — ຂອງເຈົ້າ ໜ.105
YOURS p.105 — ຂອງພວກເຈົ້າ ໜ.105

115

Indeks

A

ACT AKTO p. 2
ACTOR ARTISTA p. 50
ADULT MATANDA p. 50
AIRPLANE EROPLANO p. 67
ALLIGATOR BUWAYA p. 87
ANIMALS HAYOP p. 87
ARTIST ARTISTA p. 50
AUNT TIYA p. 64

B

BABY SANGGOL p. 51
BABYSITTER
TAGA BANTAY NG BATA p. 51
BALL BOLA p. 83
BARBER BARBERO p. 51
BASEMENT SILONG p. 71
BATHROOM BANYO p. 71
BATHTUB BANYADERA p. 71
BEAR OSO p. 87
BED KAMA p. 72
BEDROOM
SILID TULUGAN p. 72
BEE BUBUYOG p. 88
BICYCLE BISIKLETA p. 67
BIG MALAKI p. 34
BIRD IBON p. 88
BITE KAGAT p. 80
BLOOD DUGO p. 80
BOAT BANGKA p. 67
BORED NABABAGOT p. 26
BOY BATANG LALAKI p. 52
BRAVE MATAPANG p. 26
BRIGHT MALIWANAG p. 34
BROTHER
KAPATID NA LALAKI p. 64
BRUISE PASA p. 80
BUILD GUMAWA p. 2
BURN PASO p. 81
BUS BUS p. 68
BUSDRIVER
DRIBER NG BUS p. 52
BUTTERFLY PARUPARO p. 88

C

CAR KOTSE p. 68
CARPENTER KARPENTERO p. 52
CAT PUSA p. 89
CATCH SALO p. 2
CHAIR SILYA p. 72
CHASE HABULIN p. 3
CHEF
PUNONG KUSINERO p. 53
CHICKEN MANOK p. 89
CHILDREN MGA BATA p. 53
CLEAN MAGLINIS p. 3, 34
CLIMB UMAKYAT p. 3
CLOSED SARADO p. 43
CLOWN PAYASO p. 53
COLD MAGINAW p. 36
COOK TAGAPAGLUTO p. 36
COW BAKA p. 89
CRAYON KRAYOLA p. 83
CRY IYAK p. 4
CURTAIN KURTINA p. 73
CUT HIWA p. 81

D

DANCE SAYAW p. 4
DANCER MANANAYAW p. 54
DARK MADILIM p. 35
DEER USA p. 90
DENTIST DENTISTA p. 54
DIFFICULT MAHIRAP p. 36
DIG MAGHUKAY p. 5

DINOSAUR DINOSAURO p. 90
DIRTY MARUMI p. 35
DIVE SUMISID p. 5
DOCTOR DOKTOR p. 54
DOG ASO p. 90
DOLL MANIKA p. 83
DOOR PINTO p. 73
DOWN PABABA p. 47
DRAW MAGDROWING p. 5
DREAM PANAGINIP p. 6
DRESSER TUKADOR p. 73
DRINK UMINOM p. 6
DRIVE MAGAMANEHO p. 6
DRY TUYUIN p. 47
DRYER
TUYUAN NG DAMIT p. 74
DUCK BIBI p. 91

E

EASY MADALI p. 37
EAT KUMAIN p. 7
ELEPHANT ELEPANTE p. 91
EMBARRASSED
NAPAHIYA p. 26
EXCITED
TUWANG TUWA p. 27

F

FAKE HINDI TUNAY p. 43
FALL MAHULOG p. 7
FAMILY PAMILYA p. 63
FAR MALAYO p. 41
FARMER MAGBUBUKID p. 55
FAT MATABA p. 36
FATHER AMA p. 64
FEED PAKAININ p. 7
FEEL DAMAHIN p. 8
FEW KUNTI p. 41
FIND HANAPIN p. 8
FIREFIGHTER BOMBERO p. 55
FISH ISDA p. 8, 91
FISHERMAN
MANGINGISDA p. 55
FLOWER BULAKLAK p. 98
FLY LUMIPAD p. 9
FLY-A-KITE
MAGPALIPAD NG
SARANGGOLA p. 9
FOOLISH LOKO p. 27
FOX SORA p. 92
FRIEND KAIBIGAN p. 56
FRIENDLY
PALAKAIBIGAN p. 27
FROG PALAKA p. 92
FRUSTRATED BIGO p. 28
FULL BUSOG p. 38

G

GAME LARO p. 84
GARAGE GARAHE p. 74
GIRAFFE HIRAPA p. 92
GIRL BATANG BABAE p. 56
GIVE IBIGAY p. 9
GRANDFATHER LOLO p. 65
GRANDMOTHER LOLA p. 65
GRASS DAMO p. 98

H

HAPPY MALIGAYA p. 28
HARD MATIGAS p. 45
HE SIYA p. 102
HEAVY MABIGAT p. 38
HELICOPTER
HELIKOPTER p. 68
HELP TULONG p. 10
HER KANIYA p. 102

HERS KANYA p. 102
HIDE MAGTAGO p. 10
HIGH MATAAS p. 38
HIM KANIYA p. 102
HIS SA KANYA p. 102
HIT HAMPASIN p. 10
HORSE KABAYO p. 93
HOT MAINIT p. 37
HOUSE BAHAY p. 74
HUNGRY GUTOM p. 39
HURT MASAKIT p. 28

I

I AKO p. 102
ICE SKATE
ISKETING SA YELO p. 11
IN SA LOOB p. 40
IT IYAN p. 103

J

JEALOUS SELOS p. 29
JUMP TUMALON p. 11

K

KISS HALIK p. 11
KITCHEN KUSINA p. 75
KITE SARANGGOLA p. 84
KNIT MAGNITING p. 12

L

LAMP LAMPARA p. 75
LAUGH TUMAWA p. 12
LIBRARIAN LIBRARYAN p. 56
LIGHT MAGAAN p. 39
LION LEON p. 93
LIVING ROOM SALAS p. 75
LONELY NALULUMBAY p. 29
LOSE MAWALA p. 12
LOVE PAGMAMAHAL p. 13
LOW MABABA p. 39

M

MAD GALIT p. 29
MAGICIAN
SALAMANGKERO p. 57
MAILCARRIER KARTERO p. 57
MAKE GAWIN p. 13
MAN LALAKI p. 57
MANY MARAMI p. 40
ME AKO p. 102
MEAN SALBAHE p. 30
MECHANIC MEKANIKO p. 58
MICROWAVE OVEN
MIKROWAVE OBEN p. 76
MINE AKIN p. 103
MONKEY UNGGOY p. 93
MOTHER INA p. 65
MOTORCYCLE
MOTORSIKLO p. 69
MOUSE DAGA p. 94
MY AKIN p. 103

N

NEAR MALAPIT p. 40
NEIGHBOR KAPITBAHAY p. 58
NERVOUS
NINENERBYOS p. 30
NICE NAKALULUGOD p. 30
NURSE NARS p. 58

O

OLD MATANDA p. 47
OPEN BUKAS p. 42
OUR ATIN p. 103
OURS SA ATIN p. 103
OUT SA LABAS p. 41

P

PAINT PINTURA p. 13

PAINTER PINTOR p. 59
PARENTS MAGULANG p. 66
PEOPLE MGA TAO p. 59
PET ALAGANG HAYOP p. 14
PICTURE LARAWAN p. 76
PIG BABOY p. 94
PILOT PILOTO p. 59
PLANT HALAMAN p. 14, 99
PLAY MAGLARO p. 14
POISON LASON p. 81
POLICE PULIS p. 60
PRETTY MAGANDA p. 42
PROUD
LUGOD NA LUGOD p. 31
PULL HILAHIN p. 15
PUPPET PAPET p. 84
PUSH ITULAK p. 15
PUT ILAGAY p. 15

R

RABBIT KUNEHO p. 94
RACCOON
"RACCOON" p. 95
READ BUMASA p. 16
REAL TUNAY p. 42
REFRIGERATOR
REPRIDYERETOR p. 76
RIDE SUMAKAY p. 16
ROCKET RAKET p. 69
ROCKINGHORSE
LARUAN NA KABAYONG
KAHOY NA UMUUGOY p. 85
ROLL GUMULONG p. 16
ROLLERSKATE ISKET p. 17
ROW MAGSAGWAN p. 17
RUN TUMAKBO p. 17

S

SAD MALUNGKOT p. 31
SALESPERSON
TAGAPAGBILI p. 60
SANDBOX
KAHON NG BUHANGIN p. 85
SCARED NATAKOT p. 31
SCIENTIST SIYENTIPIKO p. 60
SEARCH HANAPIN p. 18
SEE TINGNAN p. 18
SEESAW SISO p. 85
SEW MANAHI p. 18
SHE SIYA p. 102
SHEEP TUPA p. 95
SHOCK PAGKABIGLA p. 82
SHORT MABABA p. 44
SHOWER MALIGO p. 77
SHY MAHIYAIN p. 32
SICK MAYSAKIT p. 44
SILLY
MAGLUKO-LUKUHAN p. 32
SINGER
MANGANGANTA p. 61
SINK LABABO p. 77
SISTER
KAPATID NA BABAE p. 66
SIT MAUPO p. 19
SKATEBOARD
ISKETBOARD p. 86
SKUNK "SKUNK" p. 95
SLED PARAGOS p. 86
SLEEP MATULOG p. 19
SLIDE PADULASAN p. 19
SMALL MALIIT p. 35
SMELL AMOYIN p. 20
SNAKE AHAS p. 96
SNOB MAPAGMATAAS p. 32

SOFA SOPA p. 77
SOFT MALAMBOT p. 44
SPIDER GAGAMBA p. 96
SPIN UMIKOT p. 20
STAND TUMAYO p. 20
STING KAGAT p. 82
STOVE KALAN p. 78
SUBWAY "SUBWAY" p. 69
SURPRISE MAGULAT p. 33
SWIM LUMANGOY p. 21
SWING SUWING p. 21

T

TABLE MESA p. 78
TAKE KUNIN p. 21
TALK MAGSALITA p. 22
TALL MATAAS p. 45
TASTE TIKMAN p. 22
TEACHER GURO p. 61
THEIR KANILA p. 104
THEIRS KANILA p. 104
THEM SA KANILA p. 104
THEY SILA p. 104
THIEF MAGNANAKAW p. 61
THIN PAYAT p. 37
THIRSTY NAUUHAW p. 33
THROW IHAGIS p. 22
TIGER TIGRE p. 96
TIP TOE PATIYAD p. 23
TIRED PAGOD p. 33
TOILET BANYO p. 78
TOYS MGA LARUAN p. 86
TRADE MAGPALITAN p. 23
TRAIN TREN p. 70
TRANSPORTATION
TRANSPORTASYON p. 70
TRASH BASURAHAN p. 79
TREE PUNO p. 99
TRUCK TRAK p. 70
TURKEY PABO p. 97
TURTLE PAGONG p. 97

U

UGLY PANGIT p. 43
UNCLE TIYO p. 66
UP PATAAS p. 46
US TAYO p. 104

V

VETERINARIAN
BETERINARYO p. 62

W

WAITRESS SERBIDORA p. 62
WALK MAGLAKAD p. 23
WASH MAGHUGAS p. 24
WASHING MACHINE
MAKINA NA PANG-LABA NG
DAMIT p. 79
WATCH MANOOD p. 24
WE KAMI p. 104
WELL MAGALING p. 45
WET BASA p. 46
WINDOW BINTANA p. 70
WOLF LOBO p. 97
WOMAN BABAE p. 62
WRITE SUMULAT p. 24

Y

YOUNG BATA p. 46
YOU IKAW p. 105
YOU ALL
KAYONG LAHAT p.105
YOUR INYO p. 105
YOURS IYO p. 105

Bảng Liet kê

A
ACT p. 2 đóng kịch
ACTOR p. 50 diễn viên
ADULT p. 50 người lớn
AIRPLANE p. 67 máy bay
ALLIGATOR p. 87 cá xấu
ANIMALS p. 87 loài vật
ARTIST p. 50 nghệ sĩ
AUNT p. 64 cô, dì, mợ

B
BABY p. 51 con nít
BABYSITTER p. 51 người coi giữ con nít
BALL p. 83 trái banh
BARBER p. 51 Thợ cắt tóc.
BASEMENT p. 71 tầng hầm
BATHROOM p. 71 phòng tắm
BATHTUB p. 71 bồn tắm
BEAR p. 87 con gấu
BED p. 72 giường
BEDROOM p. 72 phòng ngủ
BEE p. 88 con ong
BICYCLE p. 67 xe đạp
BIG p. 34 to, lớn
BIRD p. 88 chim
BITE p. 80 cắn
BLOOD p. 80 máu
BOAT p. 67 ghe, tàu
BORED p. 26 chán
BOY p. 52 con trai
BRAVE p. 26 dũng cảm
BRIGHT p. 34 trong sáng
BROTHER p. 64 anh, em(trai)
BRUISE p. 80 bầm tím
BUILD p. 2 xây, dựng
BURN p. 81 đốt
BUS p. 68 xe buýt
BUSDRIVER p. 52 tài xế xe buýt
BUTTERFLY p. 88 bướm

C
CAR p. 68 xe hơi
CARPENTER p. 52 thợ mộc
CAT p. 89 mèo
CATCH p. 2 bắt
CHAIR p. 72 ghế
CHASE p. 3 đuổi
CHEF p. 53 đầu bếp
CHICKEN p. 89 gà
CHILDREN p. 53 trẻ con
CLEAN p. 3, 34 lau chùi, sạch
CLIMB p. 3 trèo
CLOSED p. 43 đóng
CLOWN p. 53 hề
COLD p. 36 lạnh
COOK p. 4 nấu ăn
COW p. 89 bò
CRAYON p. 83 bút chì
CRY p. 4 khóc
CURTAIN p. 73 màn che cửa
CUT p. 81 cắt đứt

D
DANCE p. 4 khiêu vũ
DANCER p. 54 vũ công
DARK p. 35 đen tối
DEER p. 90 nai
DENTIST p.54 nha sĩ
DIFFICULT p. 36 khó khăn

DIG p. 5 đào
DINOSAUR p. 90 khủng long
DIRTY p. 35 dơ bẩn
DIVE p. 5 nhào lộn xuống
DOCTOR p. 54 bác sĩ
DOG p. 90 chó
DOLL p. 83 búp bê
DOOR p. 73 cửa ra vào
DOWN p. 47 ở dưới
DRAW p. 5 vẽ
DREAM p. 6 mơ mộng
DRESSER p. 73 tủ đựng quần áo
DRINK p. 6 uống
DRIVE p. 6 lái xe
DRY p. 47 khô
DRYER p. 74 máy xấy
DUCK p. 91 vịt

E
EASY p. 37 dễ dàng
EAT p. 7 ăn
ELEPHANT p. 91 con voi
EMBARRASSED p. 26 lúng túng
EXCITED p. 27 hào hứng

F
FAKE p. 43 giả tạo
FALL p. 7 mùa thu
FAMILY p. 63 gia đình
FAR p. 41 xa xôi
FARMER p. 55 nhà nông
FAT p. 36 mỡ
FATHER p. 64 cha
FEED p. 7 cho ăn
FEEL p. 8 cảm thấy
FEW p. 41 ít
FIND p. 8 tìm thấy
FIREFIGHTER p. 55 lính chữa lửa.
FISH p. 8, 91 câu cá, cá
FISHERMAN p. 55 dân chài
FLOWER p. 98 hoa
FLY p. 9 bay
FLY-A-KITE p. 9 thả diều
FOOLISH p. 27 điên rồ
FOX p. 92 con cáo
FRIEND p. 56 bạn
FRIENDLY p. 27 thân thiện
FROG p. 92 con ếch
FRUSTRATED p 28 thất vọng
FULL p. 38 no, đầy

G
GAME p. 84 trò chơi
GARAGE p. 74 nhà để xe
GIRAFFE. p. 92 hươu cao cổ
GIRL p. 56 con gái
GIVE p. 9 cho
GRANDFATHER p. 65 ông
GRANDMOTHER p. 65 bà
GRASS p. 98 cỏ

H
HAPPY p. 28 sung sướng
HARD p. 45 khó
HE p.102 nó (chủ từ giống đực)
HEAVY p. 38 nặng
HELICOPTER p. 68 trực thăng
HELP p. 10 giúp đỡ
HER p. 102 nó (giống cái)
HERS p. 102 của nó
HIDE p. 10 cất giấu
HIGH p. 38 cao
HIM p. 102 nó (giống đực)
HIS p. 102 của nó
HIT p. 10 đánh
HORSE p. 93 ngựa

HOT p. 37 nóng
HOUSE p. 74 nhà
HUNGRY p. 39 đói
HURT p. 28 làm mất lòng

I
I p. 102 tôi
ICE SKATE p. 11 trượt băng
IN p. 40 bên trong
IT p. 103 nó (trung tính)

J
JEALOUS p. 29 khen tuông
JUMP p. 11 nhảy

K
KISS p. 11 hôn
KITCHEN p. 75 bếp
KITE p. 84 con diều
KNIT p. 12 đan

L
LAMP p. 75 đèn
LAUGH p. 12 cười
LIBRARIAN p. 56 quản thủ thư viện
LIGHT p. 39 nhẹ
LION p. 93 sư tử
LIVING ROOM p. 75 phòng khách
LONELY p. 29 cô đơn
LOSE p. 12 mất
LOVE p. 13 yêu thương
LOW p. 39 thấp

M
MAD p. 29 điên dại
MAGICIAN p. 57 phù thủy
MAILCARRIER p. 57 người phát thơ
MAKE p.13 làm
MAN p. 57 đàn ông
MANY p. 40 nhiều
ME p. 102 tôi
MEAN p. 30 xấu
MECHANIC p. 58 thợ máy
MICROWAVE OVEN p. 76 lò điện
MINE p. 103 của tôi
MONKEY p. 93 khỉ
MOTHER p. 65 mẹ
MOTORCYCLE p. 69 mô tô
MOUSE p. 94 chuột
MY p. 103 của tôi

N
NEAR p. 40 gần
NEIGHBOR p. 58 hàng xóm
NERVOUS p. 30 lo lắng
NICE p. 30 tử tế
NURSE p. 58 điều dưỡng

O
OLD p. 47 già
OPEN p. 42 mở
OUR p. 103 của chúng tôi (ta)
OURS p. 103 của chúng tôi (ta)
OUT p. 41 bên ngoài

P
PAINT p. 13 sơn
PAINTER p. 59 thợ sơn
PARENTS p. 66 cha mẹ
PEOPLE p. 59 người ta
PET p.14 thú vật nuôi chơi
PICTURE p. 76 hình ảnh
PIG p. 94 heo
PILOT p. 59 phi công
PLANT p. 14, 99 trồng, cây
PLAY p.14 chơi đổn
POISON p. 81 thuốc độc
POLICE p. 60 cảnh sát

PRETTY p. 42 đẹp
PROUD p. 31 tự hào
PULL p. 15 kéo
PUPPET p. 84 con rối
PUSH p. 15 đẩy
PUT p. 15 đặt

R
RABBIT p. 94 con thỏ
RACCOON p. 95 gấu trúc
READ p. 16 đọc
READ p. 42 thật
REFRIGERATOR p. 76 tủ lạnh
RIDE p. 16 cưỡi xe đạp
ROCKET p. 69 hỏa tiễn
ROCKINGHORSE p. 85 ngựa đua
ROLL p. 16 lăn
ROLLERSKATE p. 17 đi trượt giày
ROW p. 17 chèo
RUN p. 17 chạy

S
SAD p. 31 buồn rầu
SALESPERSON p. 60 người bán hàng
SANDBOX p. 85 hố cát
SCARED p. 31 sợ sệt
SCIENTIST p. 60 khoa học gia
SEARCH p. 18 tìm tòi
SEE p. 18 nhìn
SEESAW p. 85 đu bập bênh
SEW p. 18 may
SHE p. 102 nó (chủ từ giống cái)
SHEEP p. 95 cừu
SHOCK p. 82 điện giật
SHORT p. 44 lùn
SHOWER p. 77 hoa sen tắm
SHY p. 32 e thẹn
SICK p. 44 đau ốm
SILLY p. 32 ngu xuẩn
SINGER p. 61 ca sĩ
SINK p. 77 bồn rửa
SISTER p. 66 chị, em (gái)
SIT p. 19 ngồi
SKATEBOARD p. 86 bàn trượt
SLED p. 86 xe trượt tuyết
SLEEP p. 19 ngủ
SLIDE p. 19 tuột
SMALL p. 35 nhỏ
SMELL p. 20 ngửi
SNAKE p. 96 rắn
SNOB p. 32 làm ngơ
SOFA p. 77 ghế xô pha
SOFT p. 44 mềm
SPIDER p. 96 nhện
SPIN p. 20 quay tít
STAND p. 20 đứng
STING p. 82 đau nhức
STOVE p. 78 lò bếp
SUBWAY p. 69 xe điện ngầm
SURPRISE p. 33 ngạc nhiên
SWIM p. 21 bơi lội
SWING p. 21 đánh đu

T
TABLE p. 78 cái bàn
TAKE p. 21 lấy
TALK p. 22 nói chuyện
TALL p. 45 cao lớn
TASTE p. 22 nếm

TEACHER p. 61 thầy cô
THEIR p. 104 của chúng nó
THEIRS p. 104 của chúng nó
THEM p. 104 chúng nó
THEY p. 104 chúng nó
THIEF p. 61 ăn cắp
THIN p. 37 mỏng
THIRSTY p. 33 khát nước
THROW p. 22 liệng
TIGER p. 96 cọp
TIP TOE p. 23 đi bằng năm đầu ngón chân
TIRED p. 33 mệt nhọc
TOILET p. 78 bồ vệ sinh
TOYS p. 86 đồ chơi
TRADE p. 23 trao đổi
TRAIN p. 70 xe lửa
TRANSPORTATION p. 70 chuyên chở
TRASH CAN p. 79 thùng đựng rác
TREE p. 99 cây
TRUCK p. 70 xe chở hàng
TURKEY p. 97 gà tây
TURTLE p. 97 rùa

U
UGLY p. 43 xấu xí
UNCLE p. 66 chú(bác, cậu)
UP p. 46 trên cao
US p. 104 chúng ta

V
VETERINARIAN p. 62 bác sĩ thú y

W
WAITRESS p. 62 hầu bàn (nữ)
WALK p. 23 đi bộ
WASH p. 24 giặt
WASHING MACHINE p. 79 máy giặt
WATCH p. 24 xem (coi)
WE p. 104 chúng ta
WELL p. 45 khỏe mạnh
WET p. 46 ướt
WINDOW p. 70 cửa sổ
WOLF p. 97 chó sói
WOMAN p. 62 đàn bà
WRITE p. 24 viết

Y
YOUNG p. 46 trẻ
YOU p. 105 anh(chị)
YOU ALL p. 105 tất cả anh (chị)
YOUR p. 105 của anh (chị)
YOURS p. 105 của anh (chị)

OTHER DAWNSIGNPRESS PRODUCTS